A Short History of
New Orleans

To my wife, researcher, and soul-mate,
"Nonie" Briant.

It would have been impossible to tell this story properly without the aid
of many others who share my love for the city including: Mary Lou
Christovich, Patricia Schmidt, Stanton Frazar, Collin B. Hamer, Patricia
McWhorter, Laurie Falgout, Catherine Chrestia, Bruce Sossaman, and
Edna B. Freiberg.

A Short History of New Orleans

Mel Leavitt

LEXIKOS

San Francisco

First published in July 1982 by
LEXIKOS

Edited by Lucas Myers and Tom Cole. Designed
by Craig Bergquist. Maps by Tom Dolan.
Production by Katie Meadow and Alan Magary.
Text set in Stempel Palatino by Accent &
Alphabet. Printed and bound by Malloy
Lithographing.

Front cover illustration courtesy the Historic New
Orleans Collection. A. R. Waud's 1871 wood
engraving (handcoloring added) shows the Wise
Men preparing for a parade on Canal Street; view
is southeast, toward the Mississippi River.

Library of Congress Cataloging in Publication
Data

Leavitt, Mel
    A short history of New Orleans.

    Bibliography: p.
    Includes index.
    1. New Orleans (La.)—History.   I. Title.
F379.N557L4   976.3'35   82-7138
ISBN 0-938530-03-8 (pbk.)   AACR2

        86 87 5 4

Contents

The Beginning

1

It was a harsh, forbidding place to build a city. By early springtime, armadas of mosquitoes filled the dense, subtropical air. Tough, fibrous cane sprang from the marshland, ten feet tall, excellent cover for wildlife and game. When the wind was right, you could smell the alligator musk. Water moccasins slithered silently in and out of the swampy ooze. Giant cypresses, decorated with gray, scraggly moss, stood sentinel over the dark green waters.

This was the primeval swamp as it probably appeared to those first European settlers who came here, seeking gold and pearls, less than 300 years ago. Apart from Okefenokee and the wild Everglades, there were few places more untamed or less likely to support a city in what was to be the United States. Years later, when fever, and floods, and hurricanes repeatedly threatened to destroy it, a northern engineer exclaimed: "New Orleans was built in a place God never intended a city to be built . . . six feet below sea level in the middle of a swamp, squeezed between a giant river and a huge lake. . . ." The French who settled here had a phrase for their predicament. "We live," they said, "on *Le Flottant*—The Floating Land." Other settlers called it *"La Prairie Tremblante*—The Shaking Prairie. The English shuddered and named it the Wet Grave.

Water, incredible quantities of water, was the source of its predicament, and the means of its salvation. Today, New Orleans is the only major city in the United States that lies below sea level. Of the 30 largest cities, it has the most rainfall, from 54 to 64 inches a year. It also has the mightiest free-flowing source of water, and therefore of cheap energy and water-traffic, in the nation, the Mississippi River.

"Thames and all the rivers of the kings ran into the Mississippi and were drowned." So wrote the poet Stephen Vincent Benét. The great river's awe-

Opposite page
The Swamp Forest: It was still eerily primeval when sketched in 1866 by A.R. Waud.

The Mississippi is a builder and a destroyer. The mud, sand, silt and gravel it dumps into the Gulf each *day* would fill a freight train 150 miles long. The 350 million cubic yards of top-soil carried into the delta annually would, if spread one inch thick, cover the state of Connecticut.

some power and majesty have captivated all who have come upon it. Mindful of its commercial value and strategic location, they learned to fear its brute strength and angry moods as well. The Indians called it Big River or The Father of Waters. The *sauvages*, as the French called the Indians, knew little of its ancient history or its perpetual contest with the land and swamp. They could only wonder how it created new land out of sediment—mud, silt, clay, gravel, and sand. But they could readily see the results, an ever-growing alluvial plain that stretched 600 miles northward from the Gulf.

The Mississippi is a geological upstart; its first tricklings appeared little more than one million years ago. Today, it is sustained by more than 250 tributaries, draining one-third of America's vast heartland. This great down-pouring has built up one overlapping delta after another, faster than the hungry Gulf tides could devour them. The present state of Louisiana was once entirely underwater, an enormous embayment. The sea gradually re-treated and the river advanced, filling the embayment with a series of deltaic lodes that now cover 15,000 square miles. Today, this one massive delta is overlaid by a baffling complex of distributaries, lakes, bayous, bays, marshes, and swamps. The marshland camouflages mammoth subterranean deposits of oil, natural gas, sulfur, and salt. Cavernous underground salt domes thrust out of the level swamp to form forested islands, some rising 200 feet high. There are more riches hidden beneath Louisiana's "floating land" than most other states have brought to light.

The shadowy recesses of the Louisiana swamp-forest have fascinated outlanders for centuries. Lafcadio Hearn wrote lyrically of what he called the "sombre mazes of swamp-forest." He swore that the low land "must have been rent asunder by the sea . . . strewn about the Gulf in fantastic tatters." George Washington Cable talked of the "immense wet level expanse, covered everywhere shoulder-high with marsh grasses, indented by extensive bays. . . ." The swamp-forest has also provided a splendid hiding place for smugglers, privateers, desperadoes, and alligators. That flagless captain, Jean Lafitte, established his international society of cutthroats and brigands in Barataria Bay, once, before it changed its course, the outlet of the restless Mississippi. Lafitte called it his "Back Door to New Orleans." Barataria, he insisted, meant "deception," and he was right. Most of the land was water, and the water was often barely submerged land. Deceptively submerged cypress logs sometimes looked like alligators. Submerged alligators often appeared to be trees. Seemingly bottomless channels harbored ghostly *chê-nières*, small hillocks or sudden ridges crowned by evergreen oaks. Scarcely anyone—except the Cajuns who live there and the swamp pirates and Indians who used to—has ever succeeded in navigating the phantom waterways of

Barataria.

The gnarled old cypress, brooding in the swamp-forest's murk and mist, displays large tumor-like growths just above the water line. These are the cypress knees, which literally breathe for the ancient tree. A mutant known as the dwarf cypress is a kind of troll, all undergrown and misshapen. The giant bald cypress, on the other hand, is not a cypress at all. It is a cousin of the towering California sequoia. Spanish moss, which everywhere festoons the cypress and oak trees, is related to the pineapple. This gray, stringy hanger-on was once considered a parasite, and Hearn called it a "vegetable thug." Actually, it is an epiphyte, or air-plant, and it is truly dying now, slowly asphyxiated by the growing toxicity of its food, the air. But the swamp still abounds with opulent plants and flowers: the tall tupelo and squatty palmetto, swamp red myrtle which flame briefly into gaudy magnificence, black willow, wax myrtle, wild iris, and the spider lily. The swamp is life and growth, flowering in exotic languor.

To the Choctaw, the gray-black frizzle that shrouded the bayou cypress was *iti shumo*—"tree hair." The French named the stuff *barbe a l'espagnole*—"Spanish beard." The Spanish retaliated by calling it Frenchmen's wig, and the Americans incorrectly dubbed it Spanish moss.

The River and the Isle: The Mississippi, geologically a child, did not settle in its current course until 1,000 to 500 years ago. Lake Pontchartrain was an immense intrusion of the Gulf that backed up after the Ice Age and covered 610 square miles. It, too, is relatively a youngster, barely 5,000 years old. It was on the floating morass separating these two bodies of water that Europeans began looking for a site to build a city. Between the river and the lake the Indians called "Wide Water" and we call Pontchartrain, there were two natural levees and one interrupted land ridge. All else was marshland, barely able to support the weight of a man. That marshy area trapped between the lake and river would one day become known as the "Isle of Orleans." It was water-locked and forbidding, and yet it became an obsession with the French, who understood that he who controlled the river's crescent was destined to control the great valley and its bounty.

The whole area flooded three months a year and lay uneasily on the edge of the continental shelf, lacking a rock foundation. In flood, the Mississippi became a thundering torrent, overtopping its natural levees, and overflowing hundreds of square miles of land. (Until the disastrous floods of 1927 impelled the U.S. Army Corps of Engineers to develop a comprehensive flood control plan, Old Man River did about anything he wanted.)

When the Mississippi was not boiling over man-made levees, it backlashed on them, tearing open crevasses sometimes a quarter of a mile long. In compensation, the river often deposited tons of rich, land-building silt, creating what the French called a *batture*. This created land was quickly occupied

Since the French priests who wrote the first reports transliterated freely, no one knows the exact words the Indians used for the Mississippi. Algonquins said *Miss* for "big" and *Sipi* for "water." Spelling differed as widely as it does today: Messipi, Michisipy, Misicipi.

by squatters who defied anyone to evict them from their shantytowns. One immense crevasse flooded uptown New Orleans in 1816 when it was still largely uninhabited marsh. It also laid down acres of new soil, building the foundation for what is now the city's plush Garden District. The river continually gives and takes away. One remarkable variety of willow tree is equipped by nature to survive on the *batture*. It survives because it adapts at the first sign of flooding. When the river rampages, the *batture* willow grows a new kind of root system on its upper trunk and branches. It then is able to breathe when other plants drown.

Even today, the Mississippi is cantankerous, and periodically indicates a desire to take another route. It redirects its path each year by adding or cutting off another loop or two. The river recently clipped so many loops from its meanders that its length was reduced by 50 miles. The Mississippi has created an entire natural economy out of the rich alluvial bottom land along

Columbus may have been the first European to sight the Mississippi. The maps of his fourth journey to the New World noted a "River of the Palms." That he made no further exploration is hardly surprising: the river's entrance is so treacherous that even today ocean-going skippers give way to specialists in negotiating the 100 miles upstream to New Orleans.

its valley. The lower swamps and estuaries are its natural distributaries, reaching out into the Gulf. Its deposits have enriched a nursery and harvesting ground extending far into the Gulf, which teems with fish and shellfish. The 397-mile coastline of Louisiana is an estuarian fantasy, "a curious landscape where most of the world is sky." It is so fiercely indented and dispersed, so broken into bays, bayous, inlets, and lakes, the true coastline measures an incredible 7,721 miles. It is still imperceptibly changing as Hearn wrote a century ago "more slowly, yet not less fantastically, than the clouds in heaven." An early French explorer called it "an impossible place, fit only for the jungle savage and the prehistoric crocodile." But this great delta swamp-forest and mineral-rich estuarian complex would one day yield wealth undreamed of by the first conquerors and soldiers of fortune.

The Plump Indians: If the swamp teaches anything, it teaches survival. Life moves carefully, quietly, at a measured pace. The stifling humidity smothers the impulse to hasty action. Adaptability and camouflage are natural states, ways of blending into a hostile environment where nothing is ever exactly what it seems. This is the secret of the alligator, and the lizard, the plumed bird, and the furtive water moccasin. In the swamp, all travel silently, carefully, blending in, keeping pace.

A 20-year moratorium on gator-hunting, following a century of slaughter, was lifted in 1980. Today, Antoine's, New Orleans' celebrated restaurant, serves an excellent gator soup.

The first humans to dwell in the delta marshland were semi-nomadic Indians. They moved as the river moved and the terrain shifted, responding to floods and storms, animal migrations, hostile intruders, the vicissitudes of Mother Nature and Father Mississippi. They fished the bayous and farmed the swamps for at least 10,000 years before the Europeans arrived. Ancient

A Short History of New Orleans

shell middens reveal that the first inhabitants fished for shrimp, oysters, and crabs. They lived nearly naked half the year, adapting to the torrid climate. Fish and game were plentiful, so there was no threat of a food shortage and certainly no thought of a drought. Agriculturalists and fishermen, the Indians were generally amiable, peaceful, and plump. They tattooed themselves and some flattened their children's heads with bags of sand.

Assorted jungle fevers prevented the white explorers who arrived in the 1600s from penetrating very far into the humid marsh. When the French finally settled, tentatively, they cursed the "floating land" but, with the help of the *sauvage,* they learned to live with and off it. They learned how to catch the mudfish (*choupique*) and the immense alligator gar. They discovered the original "ugly duckling," the *poule d'eau,* which ate mostly fish and tasted that way. They developed respect for the alligator, that throwback to the ichthyosaur, that looked as though it had been dozing since it first slithered out of the primeval slime. One early resident, Antoine Le Page du Pratz, wrote: "Those lakes are stored with monstrous carp, as well for size as for length... the quantity of fish... is very surprising especially as they abound among vast numbers of alligators." Seventy-seven per cent of all the species of birds known on the North American continent were seen each year above and on the delta. One half of the continent's ducks and geese passed overhead, traveling the great Mississippi flyway.

Divided by a huge lake 610 square miles in area and 24 miles wide, a giant river half a mile wide and 80 feet deep, and a baffling maze of swamps, bays, and inlets, the Choctaws never did unite, as did most tribes. Divided into four sub-tribes, unwarlike and inclined to agrarian occupations, they relied mainly on guile, accommodation, and, at times, treachery, to resist the white man or to bargain with him. There probably were no more than 3,500 Choctaws on the delta when the Frenchmen came. The white interlopers, accustomed to being outnumbered themselves, used finesse and fraternization to coexist and gain Indian support. They also needed to learn the Choctaw methods of survival in the muggy swamp.

In the piney forests beyond Lake Okwata ("Wide Water," Lake Pontchartrain), the Choctaw felled loblolly pines for wood. They gathered sinewy reeds from the Buchwa ("Squeezing Bayou," now Bayou La Combe). They enjoyed a tea made from the sassafras plant, which they also ground into a pungent powder that inflamed the tongue. The French loved it and called it *filé,* the basis for their culinary inspiration, in concert with African cooks, *filé* gumbo. The Indians navigated the treacherous, uncharted waterways in dugout canoes, hand-hewn from the "eternal cypress." Their delicately balanced, shallow-draft pirogues (or *paraguas*) could deftly slip through dense over-

"King and Queen of the Mississippi": This 18th-century Dutch engraving was based on third– or fourth–hand information.

grown channels at times only six inches deep.

Some observers, influenced by naive early European accounts of "naked, cowardly, dirty savages," ridiculed the native swamp-dwellers. In much the same way, the swamp-dwelling Cajun French who arrived in the 1750s were deprecated. The French townfolk, the Creoles, derided their rural, unsophisticated manner, their fractured French, a two-century-old patois, and their lusty attachment to outdoor life, hunting, fishing, and work. The first New Orleans settlers were mainly bourgeois city people or urban grifters, steadfastly opposed to any kind of physical toil.

It's doubtful the Indians were overly industrious in the enervating subtropical clime. One historian flatly states that the Choctaw were "the only lazy Indians," and that despite their proficiency with pirogues and other watercraft, they never learned to swim. Since their record for survival is excellent, one must assume they knew how to float. There is evidence that the Choctaw built settlements on and around present-day New Orleans' "Beautiful Crescent" before the French arrived. Three hundred fifty families of the Houmas sub-tribe lived in simple huts with wooden frames, covered with palmetto leaves on a ridge near what is now St. Louis Cemetery #3, off Esplanade Avenue. By 1720, they had gone. The Colapissa lived near what is now City Park. They left to escape the warring Chickasaw. The wandering Biloxi occupied their abandoned huts, and later, following the first great flooding of the French settlement, white colonists inhabited the Indians' lodging temporarily.

The delta landscape was cluttered with Choctaw names, and the French adapted many of the more descriptive ones. The Boque Falaya is pure Choctaw and means "Long Swamp." The Castine Bayou is named after the tiny *kastni* fleas that infest the area. The most common word, bayou, is an adaptation of the Choctaw *bayuk*. This term identifies the long, narrow, singularly sluggish waters that interlace the swamp. Many Choctaw names embellish today's map of south Louisiana and New Orleans: Tangipahoa, Ponchatoula, Tchefuncta (Tiny Chestnut), Abita Springs (literally Springs Springs), Bayou Chitto, Bayou Goula, Houma, and Tchoupitoulas. Essentially farmers and fishermen, the natives prompted an early Dutch surveyor, Bernard Romans, to observe: "The Choctaw Indians may properly be called a nation of farmers, more than any savages I have met."

The Choctaw were among the most flexible of Indians; later, they became part of the so-called Five Civilized Tribes of the Southeast. They constantly modified their ways to coexist with the white man, and eventually developed an alphabet, a written language, and other trappings of civilization. One of their great chiefs, Pushmataha, fought with the Americans and was buried

Properly speaking, a Creole is a white person born in the U.S. Gulf States or the West Indies and descended from early French or Spanish settlers. A second-generation Cajun in Louisiana might fit this definition but not the reality; confusion of Creole and Cajun would be met with scorn in New Orleans.

Louisiana placenames are a source of delight for map readers. The town of Waterproof is subject to frequent floods. Cut Off is precise: there is nothing beyond but the swamp. Westwego was the terminus of the railroad going West to Texas. English Turn commemorates a Frenchman's bluff that fooled British ships into retreat.

with military honors. A New Orleans Jesuit priest, Father Adrien Rouquette, founded seven missions in the Ozone country east of Lake Pontchartrain. He became so captivated by their reverence for life that he took an Indian name, Chata Ima ("He Who is Like the Choctaw").

The Choctaw developed great respect for their fellow survivors in the steaming delta swamp. The *choupique,* or mudfish, fascinated them. Astonishingly tough, it was able to breathe air in the same manner as the gar. Both adapted to life in what is practically liquid mud along bayous and rivers. The Choctaw and the early settlers looked upon the mudfish as a kind of totem, symbolic of their battle to endure. The *choupique* still endures in south Louisiana; they have been plowed up in lowland fields after flood waters subsided, still alive. The Houmas worshipped the lowly crayfish. He moved backwards to go forwards and was superb at crawling sideways even when appearing not to move at all. The Houmas also considered the chicken sacred and refused to kill it or eat it.

Upon first encountering Choctaws, Europeans were repelled by their facial tattoos, their apparent indolence, and their filth. Choctaws bathed daily but they were in the habit of standing directly in fire-smoke at night to drive off mosquitoes. When they emerged from the smoke, they were blackened, head to toe. The Choctaw developed an effective mosquito repellent, bear fat. They were described by one early settler as "the only ugly Indians in Louisiane" and certainly the "smelliest." Some of the first colonials were cold-blooded Canadians, Quebecois, accustomed to stepping vigorously, if only to avoid frostbite. But prolonged exposure to the steaming swamp made them almost as languid as the natives. The vicious mosquitoes, the sudden tropical gales, the uncertain water currents, the uncertain ground, the suffocating heat and hostile animals all dictated caution and reserve.

La Salle's Lost Colony: The first official governor of Louisiana was René Robert Cavalier, Sieur de La Salle. "Governor" was largely an honorary title; as yet, La Salle had discovered only the river's mouth. He named it the River St. Louis in homage to his patron Louis XIV, and designated all the land constituting the western watershed *Louisiane.* Unfortunately, the youthful explorer did not live to claim it. His life's ambition was to "colonize and civilize" the Mississippi Valley. To this end La Salle's historic trip began on February 6, 1682, when he entered the big river's main channel from the Illinois. With him traveled a small party of 56 people, including 10 Indian women and three children. Two months later, they arrived at the Gulf. La Salle planted an iron cross in the mud by the river's mouth. At 39 years of

For God, King Louis, and France: La Salle claims the mighty river and its vast watershed.

A. Ft. Mobile
B. Ft. Maurepas (Biloxi)
C. Natchitoches
D. Malbouche
E. Matagorda Bay
F. New Orleans
G. The Mississippi

The first European to cross the Mississippi was the Spaniard Hernando De Soto, in 1541. He ravaged the tribes of Central and South America looking for gold, and was still looking when he died, aged 42, somewhere above Baton Rouge.

age he became the first European to track the course of the Mississippi and link De Soto's discoveries near the mouth to those of Joliet and Marquette in its upper waters.

By now France was at war with Spain, and King Louis felt a fortified colony at the river's end would be strategically important. The King supplied La Salle with four ships, about 400 men, and ample provisions. La Salle was dispatched by way of the Caribbean to relocate the river's mouth and establish a settlement. The voyage still fascinates historians. From the moment the expedition set off, La Salle and his naval commander, Beaujeu, were at each other's throat. Their main supply ship was captured by the Spanish before they reached the Indies. The two leaders squabbled so heatedly that, somehow, the entire flotilla passed right by the mouth of the Mississippi. La Salle insisted they continue another 400 miles and put in at Matagorda Bay, in what is now Texas. The landing was a disaster. A tropical storm sank one vessel, and another ship ran aground. For reasons still obscure, if not sinister, Beaujeu sailed the sole remaining seaworthy vessel back to France. La Salle and his party were stranded.

With only 45 men left and most of his supplies lost, the 44-year-old explorer kept his colony alive for almost two years in the wilderness. He built a fort which he named St. Louis and twice set out on foot, wandering cross-country in the forlorn hope of reaching Canada. La Salle finally divided his unwilling colony, leaving 25 men behind to literally "hold the fort." Then he set off northward with his Huron Indian aide and hunter, Nika, his servant, Saget, and 14 others, determined to reach Quebec, over 1,500 miles away. But his journey was no more than a few miles long. On March 18, 1687, La Salle was ambushed and killed by two mutineers. Earlier, while he was away scouting, the killers had split the skulls of his nephew, his Indian guide, and his servant while they slept by the fireside.

"Governor" La Salle's settlement disappeared. Whether they were victimized by Indians, starvation, disease, or Spaniards, no one knows for certain. Fortunately, one of the four survivors of that awful expedition, Henri Joutel, found his way back overland to the Mississippi. He smuggled out a personal diary that provided many clues to young La Salle's betrayal. In 1697, Henri de Tonti, a friend, published *La Salle's Last Discoveries in America.*

Louis XIV's dream of an American empire was reawakened when his colonial rival, Spain, claimed all the territory bordering the Gulf of Mexico, based on 180-year-old discoveries purportedly made by Pinedo. "Exploration without occupation means nothing!" proclaimed the Sun King, who then launched another three-nation race for conquest. Spain, France, and England quickly converged on the Caribbean, grasping for control of the big river, and the unnamed, unfounded city at its end.

Thirteen years after La Salle's disappearance, the brothers Le Moyne, Iberville and Bienville, set sail for the New World. Their mission was to establish a fort in the King's Colony of *Louisiane.* which loosely embraced most of the Mississippi Gulf Coast, find the missing Mississippi River, and chart it. France now realized the elusive big river must be secured. The two brothers were Quebecois, members of an illustrious family sired by a strapping Norman, Charles Le Moyne.

Le Moyne had made a fortune in the Canadian province, became a nobleman, and reared 11 children, eight of whom became distinguished military leaders. Pierre, Sieur de Iberville, was the oldest, the first soldier of all Canada at 38, and the first Canadian commissioned in the Royal French Navy. Many settlers who accompanied him to *Louisiane* were seasoned frontiersmen, Canadian grandsons of those pioneers who settled Quebec in 1608, 12 years before the landing at Plymouth Rock.

Father of New Orleans: Bienville — explorer, founder, planner, warrior, governor for 31 years.

The younger brother, Bienville, was, in the embroidered manner of the *ancien régime,* Jean Baptiste Le Moyne, Sieur de Bienville. He was a midshipman in the Royal French Navy, a stripling of 17. A third member of the party was a missionary priest, Father Anastase Douay, one of the four survivors of La Salle's ill-fated adventure. They knew that La Salle's friend, Henri de Tonti, had left a verifying letter with the Bayougoula Indians, supposedly deposited near the river's terminus along with his coat of Montreal blue. Father Douay was almost certain to recognize the coat, and the letter would establish definitely that they had rediscovered the Mississippi.

Iberville's expedition included four ships, 100 soldiers, and about 200 audacious settlers. They stopped briefly at the old sugar stronghold of Saint-Domingue on the island of Hispaniola, and then headed straight for the Florida Gulf Coast. At Pensacola, Iberville sighted land — and a Spanish party busily erecting an outpost. The Frenchmen continued west, along a snow-white beach, so dazzling in the fierce sunlight it burned the eyes. Two days later, the French flotilla came upon a small island. Iberville was ready to name it Dauphin, after the royal heir apparent. He changed his mind when he waded ashore. The tiny spit of sand and marsh grass was strewn with human skulls and bones. He named it Massacre Island instead. Later he would build a fort there called Louis de Mobile overlooking the sparkling blue-green bay, named Mobile, after a local tribe known as the Mauvila.

Saint-Domingue (called Santo Domingo by the Spanish) was the proudest possession of the French Empire. Ceded to France in 1697, it produced two-thirds of France's imports, a frenzied anismistic Afro-Caribbean religion called Voudon, and the bloodiest black revolution in history.

Iberville's curiosity propelled him further west, following a string of barrier islands. He named them, in order, Ship, Horn, and Cat. Cat Island proved a misnomer; the "cats" the crew saw frisking on the strand were actually raccoons, never seen before by these Europeans.

First Mardi Gras: Strangely enough, Iberville's first settlement was not in Louisiana as we know it today. It was near Biloxi, Mississippi.

All but 50 members of the party encamped, and the brothers Le Moyne set out in smaller craft, braving a Gulf storm, determined to find the Malbouche, so called because the Indians termed it "the Bad Mouth." This angry, swirling, rock-impeded entrance was the elusive front door to the Mississippi. That stormy night New Orleans history began, in the larger sense, as the Iberville expedition ploughed through gale winds, driving rain, and lightning, bumping invisible logs and snags, rocks and sawyers cluttering the Malbouche (now the North Pass). Exhausted, they camped a short way upstream near the entrance of a bayou. It was Mardi Gras night, 1699. The first place names given Louisiana were, appropriately, Pointe de Mardi Gras and Mardi Gras Bayou.

The next day they headed upstream in search of the Bayougoula Indians and the Speaking Bark, where Tonti's letter supposedly was hidden. Father Douay identified the first Indians they met as Choctaws by their long raven hair, their facial tattoos, and their flat heads. Near the site of the present town of Bayou Goula, the Frenchmen confirmed their rediscovery of the Mississippi. Tonti's letter had been preserved inside the hollow of a tree, "The Speaking Bark." So had his coat, the distinctive blue wool jacket with pewter buttons worn by all Montreal militiamen.

The Quebecois were jubilant; they were also susceptible to some wily Choctaw self-promotion. The Bayougoula chief assured them that his Indians knew Father Mississippi's moods better than anyone. The perfect spot for the first French settlement would be just above the Bayougoula village. To his regret later on, Iberville made special note of this.

Those first 80 miles the Le Moyne brothers paddled against the untamed Mississippi must have been awesome. The river was dark-brownish, colored with the mud and silt of a hundred smaller streams, carrying in its sweep branches and bushes and occasionally whole trees, as it careened downward toward the open Gulf. One can only imagine what the teenager Bienville thought as they mounted the great flood and swept into the majestic bend — Bienville would later refer to it as "the Beautiful Crescent" — of his future city, New Orleans. The Indians showed them a portage above the crescent, leading overland to a bayou (presently Bayou St. John), tranquil as a looking glass. It joined a great body of brackish water, very shallow and a half-day wide, called Okwata or "Wide Water" (Lake Pontchartrain). Two days further upriver, the Indians pointed out the *manchac*, or "pass," through which they could return to their Gulf base, saving two months' time. Further on, 80 miles above the crescent, they sighted a crimson pole on the east bank. Iberville dubbed it Baton Rouge ("Red Stick").

There was no doubt that this was La Salle's lost Mississippi. They turned around and headed back, using the Indian *manchac* that connected with the lake. Triumphant, Iberville named the *manchac* Iberville River and gave Okwata the name of his patron, Louis de Pontchartrain, the Minister of the Marine. This giant body of water led through Lake Borgne and on into the Gulf of Mexico. For years, it offered a much shorter alternate route for smaller craft seeking the upper Mississippi.

Iberville, impatient to reach France with his momentous report, built a fort at Biloxi within two weeks and called it Maurepas, after Pontchartrain's son. Thus the first Louisiana colony was established in Mississippi. Service to his king was the gallant Iberville's vocation. He was eager to secure the great river, but the king was a suspicious man, perpetually getting embroiled in wars he could ill afford. Iberville made the long trip to the little colony on the white sands twice more. Then Queen Anne's War took him away for good. He again distinguished himself in battle as a Navy Commander and was headed back for Louisiana when he became ill while anchored in Havana Bay. In July of 1706, he died in his cabin of yellow fever, the disease destined to become the scourge of the Crescent City.

Louis XIV (1638–1715) dominated European politics and he harbored ambitions of conquering Europe. He fought four major wars, purged France of 200,000 Protestant Huguenots, and built Versailles. His 72 years of absolute monarchy ("L'état, c'est moi") nearly bankrupted France, and hindered Louisiana's growth.

The Boy Commander: When young Bienville took charge of the Louisiana colony in 1701, following his brother's departure, he was 20 years old. Some sneered at his youth and called him "The Boy Commander." Calamity beset Bienville from the start. His settlers could not adapt to the climate or the poor soil. They died almost as quickly as new recruits arrived. The indomitable Henri de Tonti and other rugged Canadian pioneers joined him, but the miserable outpost was abandoned. The Frenchmen moved eastward and built another outpost overlooking Mobile Bay.

In 1704, the Bishop of Quebec dispatched 23 young women to the Mobile colony to provide wives for its men. The colonists were exultant, but the women quickly showed a distaste for Indian maize, or corn, and threatened to leave the colony unless they could have French bread. Bienville's gifted housekeeper, Madame Langlois, took the lady rebels aside and introduced them to the secrets of grinding meal for cornbread and preparing hominy and grits and succotash, and the rebellion was soon abandoned.

Bienville's food problems were not all so frivolous. The sandy Gulf Coast littoral is generally infertile. Supply from France was undependable, and provisions were many months in arriving. Bienville tried to alleviate periodic privation by sending his men on extended hunting trips, to live as best they

The French controlled and populated Quebec for a century and a half despite three British attempts to capture it. It was the staging ground for La Salle and other Frenchmen who moved into the Mississippi Valley. During Louisiana's colonial development, the Bishop of Quebec and his Church were the brain and heart of New France.

could among the Indians. In 1707, the situation was relieved when a large supply ship arrived. However, some of his hunters had grown to prefer the outdoor life, the bounties of bear, buffalo, duck, and snow geese, and they didn't want to return. Bienville solved his problem by announcing that the new ship had brought Bordeaux wine. "The excellent French wine," wrote the master carpenter André Penigault, "consoled us for the loss of favors of the girls . . . who were angered at our long trips hunting."

Discontent plagued Bienville throughout his Mobile adventure. Many settlers came, believing there was gold and silver, and found nothing but seashells, seaweed, and hurricanes. Other townfolk and trappers resisted toiling in the humid fields. Crops were not planted. The Indians grew hostile. Malaria and dysentery infected Bienville's company. Men greatly outnumbered women and fought over them. The colonists bickered and took sides, for or against the Boy Commander. Rumors spread that the limited stores in the warehouse on Dauphin Island were being sold at six times their cost "by those in command." The imperious Jean Baptiste Martin d'Artaguette d'Iron, who would become commissary for the province, arrived from France to investigate the charge. In short order, Bienville, the Boy Commander, was fired.

It is interesting to speculate on what might have happened if Bienville's career as a French civil servant had ended at this point. In the 41 years he served as full-time, part-time, or sometime Governor of Louisiana, he was repeatedly in hot water with someone, for personal or political reasons. Fate intervened on this occasion. The official appointed to take Bienville's place died at sea, en route to Louisiana. Bienville was reprieved and he stayed on long enough to move his quarrelsome colony to another site beyond Mobile Bay. It was a familiar story in colonial Louisiana—recurring high water and constant flooding had made the old fort untenable. In 1712, Bienville was relieved of his command and his title. The King was fed up with petty politics—it was time to put the colony in the hands of merchants, traders, and men of commerce who would brook no foolishness and make it pay.

The shrewd, peasant-born Antoine Crozat, Marquis de Chatel, was given a 15-year charter to the distant province. Crozat had profited greatly from the lucrative slave trade through his stock in the Guinea and Asiento companies. Louisiana retained a governor, the irascible founder of Detroit, Antoine Cadillac, who insulted almost every colonist before he and Louisiana mutually agreed to live without each other. Bienville was demoted to Lieutenant-Governor. He bided his time, observing Cadillac's cultivation of enemies and repeated attempts to grow grapes. Crozat, however, owned the franchise, and he ran the colony.

The **Perfect Spot:** Dreams of empire impelled hot-blooded men to search the mid-American wilderness, skirt the blue Gulf's beaches, and strike out through the swamp looking for the perfect spot near the river's mouth to found a great city. Such a city, a New Paris perhaps, could control the Mississippi watershed and the commerce of the entire continent. Twice, provisional outposts on the Mississippi coast were abandoned, victims of storm and flood. It took 36 years finally to locate on the river, at the spot the charming Bayougoula Indians recommended, 18 leagues from the river's mouth.

In 1702, Iberville erected a small fort just above the Bayougoula village. It was inundated by tropic rains and river flooding, and besieged by bloodsucking "skeeters." It turned out the Bayougoula were not experts on flood control or the river's behavior. They merely wanted an armed buffer against their enemies to the north. Iberville relocated two years later near the junction of Bayou Choupique (Bayou St. John) and Lake Pontchartrain. His settlement was called Fort St. Jean and predated the city of New Orleans by 14 years. (The ruins of the old Spanish fort can still be seen on the site.) It is the oldest permanent site in the state, located "beyond the insulting reach of floods."

Alexandre de Rémonville in his *Historical Letters Concerning the Mississippi* said the city "ought to be built on high ground dominating Lake Pontchartrain." By 1709, François de Mandeville was writing that the portage to Bayou Choupique was four or five miles above the bend (the crescent) and was "greatly advantageous." Most agreed that the bayou-portage site was superior. A riverfront site and river port seemed foolish; the unpredictable Mississippi constantly rampaged, and sometimes it took weeks just to battle 80 miles upriver. How much better to use the bypass through Lakes Pontchartrain and Borgne than brave the river's treacherous mouth "twenty leagues down a very difficult country, often flooded and filled with alligators, serpents, and other venomous beasts."

The future founder, Bienville, did not go on record until 1709. Despite every contrary opinion and every learned judgment, Bienville determined that the city's "future" was where the river's "beautiful Crescent comes closest to the Lake." He had fallen in love with the river, the crescent, and Bayou Choupique. Jean Baptiste Le Moyne, Sieur de Bienville, decided to immortalize himself while he had the chance. Bayou Choupique became Bayou St. Jean (after his patron saint, of course).

New Orleans, slow abuilding, now ranks first in the United States in the amount of cargo handled. Big Easy bests the Big Apple in the battle for primacy. Its only major industries — and they are giants — are the port and tourism. The annual human traffic is tremendous: six million visitors in a recent year.

The Founding

2

John Law was the ultimate contradiction: a Scotsman who thrived on professional gambling, a banker who preached easy credit and deficit spending. He always played for big stakes, and in 1715 the jackpot was Louisiana.

A self-promoting financial genius, Law escaped Great Britain after killing a prominent man in a duel over a lady. For 15 years, the fugitive financier toured the capitals of Europe, gambling, womanizing, and developing his master plan. He bragged that some of his information was obtained from "inside sources." European financiers branded him a "shameless manipulator," and said the "sources" were lovelorn wives of Dutch bankers.

In France, the regent, Philippe of Orleans, was a perfect mark. The Sun King, Louis XIV, had died at the age of 78, leaving his five-year-old grandson, the dauphin, head of state and the nation 64 million livres in debt. Louis' dissolute son-in-law, Philippe, became French regent and caretaker of the Empire—including Louisiana. Philippe's mother once said her son was endowed "with all talents except the talent to know how to use them." A cynic, rakehell, and probably an alcoholic, Philippe relieved the monotony of Versailles' programmed pleasures by staging impromptu orgies of his own. He was devilishly bright, bold, and determined not to be a victim of ennui. Appropriately, he and the Scots gambling man discovered each other in a Paris casino. John Law supposedly carried a bag of gold under each arm, a guaranteed ice-breaker.

Law's visionary scheme—later known as *le Mississippi* or the Mississippi Bubble— called for combining the Royal Bank with a colossal land speculation company, the Company of the West. Supported by an army of shareholders, both noble and middle-class, this grand enterprise would open that great port at the mouth of the Mississippi and extract from its valley moun-

One of history's great flim-flam men, John Law was orphaned at 14, falling heir to a fortune he quickly gambled away. London's Drury Lane Theatre once "honored" him with a tongue-in-cheek performance of Ben Jonson's "The Alchemist."

Opposite page
Early media hype: John Law promoted *le Mississippi* with a poster showing mountains, a deep-water port, adoring Indians bearing silver and gold, all imaginary.

The El Dorado mystique had mesmerized Europeans for a century. John Law's media hype was so extravagant that the Louisiana province was dubbed "The New Peru." New Orleans' daffy city seal reflects Law's fanciful descriptions. The seal features a beguiling, Europeanized maiden and towering mountains. In fact, the city's high point is a 12-foot-tall man-made hill in Audubon Park.

tains of gold and silver, acres of diamonds, emeralds, and pearls. The royal debt would magically evaporate. All France would become stockholders in John Law's brave new world.

On May 2, 1716, John Law signed a contract with the government of France. As a modest beginning he was given a mandate to establish a private bank, tacitly underwritten by the Duke of Orleans. Philippe's lifelong enemies, the royal bastards Toulouse and Burgundy, chewed fingernails watching the Scotsman's money machine generate instant credit. France's old *financières* went into shock.

Then Antoine Crozat, the disgusted proprietor of Louisiana, came home. He uttered imprecations against the floods and storms, "the voracious mosquitoes and crocodiles." Crozat said he was through looking for diamonds and pearls. In five years, he had spent four times his original investment, and had nothing to show for it but insect bites and an empty wallet. At some point, after John Law entered the discussion, the wilderness speculator told the Scotsman: "You cannot succeed!"

Crozat's warning only strengthened John Law's determination. This was his opportunity. Within six months, his land of milk and money, his El Dorado on the Mississippi, was on the drawing board. As Bienville bided his time 5,000 miles away, John Law was awarded the trade monopoly for Louisiana. Jean Michiele, Seigneur de Lepinay et de la Longueville, had replaced the argumentative, foppish Cadillac, and proven a pitifully inefficient governor. John Law, professional gambling man, could size a person up in the course of one "hand." Bienville was the man he wanted for the founder's job, and no one else. On September 20, 1717, Lepinay was replaced by the veteran explorer, now 37 years old.

There was an immediate stampede of speculators, anxious to get in on the bonanza. It became perhaps the most monumentally fraudulent real estate scheme in history. Law designed a brilliant publicity campaign, a media assault unlike anything Europe had seen before. He turned out giant posters and handbills, circulars and broadsides, depicting the pastoral glories of a land his artists invented. A nubile Indian maiden, dressed like a Grecian goddess, one breast exposed, waited with her handsome brave as a stalwart Frenchman proffered beads and trinkets. In return, the copy noted, these friendly savages most eagerly would exchange pure gold.

Law's psychology anticipated P. T. Barnum. He gave "the suckers" a vision of El Dorado. The bubble grew. Later, Montesquieu noted: "All those who were rich six months ago are now in the depth of poverty, and those who had not even bread, are swollen with riches... Never have the two extremes of our society met so closely."

The Persistent Governor: Bienville could have exposed Law. His knowledge of the territory far exceeded that of any other individual. And he was actually building Louisiana. In 1716, he built Fort Rosalie, up the river among the Natchez Indians. The fertile land in time attracted some 300 settlers, and later provoked a bloody massacre that touched off the delta's first extended Indian war.

As governor and troubleshooter in a scattered province dependent on France for supplies, Bienville endured the wrath of frustrated settlers, government spies, and political connivers, and stuck to his goal of producing another Paris in the marsh.

Everyone had some better idea. A naval officer promoted English Turn for its excellent cove and location half-way up the river. Many favored Fort Rosalie (Natchez) for its flood-free soil and commanding view from the towering bluffs. Many liked Manchac (Iberville River), 70 miles upstream, connecting the river and the two lakes. It was higher, drier, healthier. Biloxi and Mobile, the "Establishment" of the time, opposed anything on the river that took commerce away from them.

In retrospect, it seems a miracle that Bienville kept the colony alive for 20 years. Cadillac went back to Paris, having alienated every soul he met, complaining that the jungle climate was oppressive and that nothing worthwhile would grow there. His 29 vines had produced eight bunches of grapes, all of them withered. Bienville's repeated insistence that there were no gold and silver mines in Louisiana was discounted. He urged Crozat and the French government to cease searching for treasure and develop agriculture. Instead, Law's promotion became even more cloudcuckoolandish. Nobles, eager to obtain the large, rich plantation concessions upstream, went along with the scam, blathering of unlimited treasures and docile Indians eager to enter servitude.

The 37-year-old governor talked of locating a port city two days' sail from the Gulf, the next "important center of trade" in the New World. Where? His determination had not wavered since his first recommendation to Paris in 1708. But the "proposed city of New Orleans," named for the Duke of Orleans, was on French maps six months before a single tree was felled. There was no specific location; John Law and his land-speculators merely wanted a point of reference in promoting their great treasure hunt.

In Bienville's mind, the new city must be built upon an elevated tract of land, 10 feet above the Mississippi River which it fronted. It would overlook that most "beautiful crescent of the river" where it swept by only five miles from the lake, not too far from the river's mouth but far enough to escape the worst blasts of a tropical hurricane. Some four miles above his site was the

Sailing ships, forced to tack incessantly against the wind, sometimes took weeks to reach New Orleans from the river's mouth.

ancient Indian portage leading to the navigable Bayou St. John. The bayou connected in turn with Lake Pontchartrain, Lake Borgne, and the Gulf of Mexico. It was not Law's fanciful El Dorado/Eden. But it would become the "Gateway to the Americas."

Bienville suspected that Parisian politics would never permit so reasoned and practical a decision. When ships arrived at Dauphin Island (Massacre Island had reverted to this name) on March 9, 1718, bearing Bienville's official appointment, he immediately assigned 80 men to clear the ground and begin constructing houses where New Orleans now stands. For three months, his Paris employers knew nothing of his choice of land. They dispatched an engineer with instructions, but he died en route. When the message finally reached Bienville, it recommended Manchac (Bayou Iberville) as the location. Bienville reacted coyly. He'd pushed the job too far now to turn back. New Orleans had been founded on the site he chose.

Marc Antoine Hubert, commissary for the province, was dispatched to keep an eye on him. Bienville's motley crew of prisoners, carpenters, saw-yers, and slaves was working so obsessively battling cypress stumps and 12-foot cane, they'd taken time to build only one hut—Bienville's headquarters. Hubert shared it for awhile and then, disgusted, he left for Natchez where he did everything in his power to make that city the new capital.

The core of Bienville's reluctant work crew was a group of 80 convicted salt-smugglers. Many of the earliest settlers were French prisoners given their choice of imprisonment in France or freedom (of sorts) in the New World. When most chose French jails, they were forcibly sent to Louisiana to slash through canebrakes in the burning sun or contend with venomous snakes, alligators, and torrential downpours. In early June, Bienville wrote to his Parisian patrons: "We are working at New Orleans with as much zeal as the shortage of working men will allow. I have myself conveyed over the spot to select the place where it will be best to locate the settlement. I remained ten days to hasten the works . . . I am grieved to see so few people engaged in a task which requires at least a hundred times that number." Bienville went on at length, extolling the salubrious climate, the fertile soil, and its obvious advantages over "other sites." Here was the Founder, defending his decision to ignore his patrons' orders, and at the same time, complaining about their lack of support.

By now, John Law's Mississippi Scheme had become the talk of Europe. Systematically, Law took over the national bank, then trade monopolies in the far-flung French Empire—Canada, the West Indies, Africa, even Cathay. Frenchmen, noble and base-born, mortgaged or sold their homes to seek fortunes either as speculators in the Company's wildly fluctuating stock or as homesteaders, miners, prospectors, pioneers.

The commandant at Nachitoches, a settlement up the Red River where a fort had been built in 1714, complained that Bienville's sodden village was "situated in flat and swampy ground fit only for growing rice; river water filters through under the soil and crayfish abound . . . there are frequent fogs and, the land being thickly wooded and covered with canebrakes, the air is fever-laden, and an infinity of mosquitoes cause further inconvenience in summer." But John Law was too good a poker player for penny-ante politics. He had bet on Bienville from the beginning and he would back him to the end. In October 1718, the Company of the West approved the location of Nouvelle Orleans, 30 leagues (110 miles) above the mouth of the Mississippi.

New Orleans' first crude log houses, patterned after the local Choctaw huts, did not last very long. They either rotted in the damp heat· or they cracked and tilted, eventually collapsing in undignified heaps. Even today it is chancy to build wooden foundations or frames on New Orleans ground. The first mud streets, reinforced ineffectually with shells, often resembled canals. Flooding was a regular occurrence and every year most of the Isle of Orleans was a lake for as long as three months. In March 1719, the chronicler, citizen Antoine Le Page du Pratz, came down from his residence on Bayou St. John and was astonished. "It is only marked out by a hut covered with palmetto leaves," he wrote, "which Bienville had caused to be built for his own lodgings."

The first settlers arrived in three ships, accompanied by 500 soldiers and convicts. All but 68 went on to Natchez and Yazoo River country. The others crowded into tents and rough sheds. If New Orleans was here to stay, which seemed doubtful, then so were they.

The Settling: Father Pierre François-Xavier de Charlevoix, the peripatetic priest, wrote his impressions of New Orleans three years after its shaky beginnings. His narrative is breezy, and almost satirical, in light of John Law's promotional fantasy. "Here I am in the famous city they call New Orleans," he writes. "The 800 houses and five parishes which the *Mercure* attributed to it two years ago are reduced today to a hundred huts placed without much order, to a large warehouse of wood, two or three houses which would not embellish a village in France, to half of a wretched warehouse that they have consented to assign to the Lord and of which He had hardly taken possession before they wanted Him to leave it to lodge in a tent."

Antoine du Pratz remarked that it "was a town in name only." Du Pratz

Louisiana was painfully isolated from France. The voyage took six months, and colonists were lucky to see a ship every three months. The governor was harassed by belated decress, *lettres de cachet*, and prying bureaucrats.

The approved local pronunciation of "New Orleans" — how a broadcaster would say it — is *New OR-lee-uns*, but this is by no means widespread. The informal, colloquial, workingman's, or "Ninth Ward accent" renders the name as *N'AW-linz* or *N'OR-linz*, depending on where the speaker might be from originally (South or Midwest, respectively). Down home talk like this is called Yat, as in "Hey, Tom, where y'at?" The pronunciation that raises local hackles is *New Or-LEENS*, as sung in "Way Down Yonder (in New Orleans)" — composed here! "Louisiana" should be pronounced with all its syllables, as most outlanders do, but upstate it's *LOOZY-ana*. First-time visitors to the city are usually surprised that Orleanians don't talk like Southerners; in fact, many sound Brooklyn-born.

landed at Dauphin Island on August 25, 1718, along with the 67 other pioneer citizens. The Mississippi Company told them to live within the limits of New Orleans and raise gardens and, if they developed the land, they would receive larger concessions along the river. Du Pratz settled along the Bayou St. John, as did some other small landholders. He bought an Indian slave to cook his meals. One night, a 12-foot alligator moseyed in the front door, hypnotized by the fire. The slave girl slammed him hard on the snout with a broomstick and the reptile fled. Du Pratz also discovered that the hungry mosquitoes could be driven away by burning brimstone each morning and evening. Unfortunately, the fumigation process made such a stench inside that, du Pratz recalled, he had to wait an hour outside, being bitten all the time.

Bienville, the Founder, had other problems. His predominantly male colony was reinforced by a number of cutthroats, thieves, and smugglers. They were growing desperate for female companionship. Bienville wrote the king, imploringly: ''My Frenchmen are lonely. They are running in the woods after girls. Send us some women.'' The King obliged by opening the doors of a Paris prison. It was not easy to recruit cultured damsels to amuse riverfront ruffians. So, being a pragmatist, the regent Philippe shipped him 88 inmates from La Salpêtrière, a house of correction in Paris.

Nineteen of the so-called ''correction girls'' married enroute to Louisiana, and 10 died. A bibulous midwife, Madame Doville, called la Sans Regret, *came along just in case.*

The Pest Flotillas: As word of the sultry reality of New Orleans filtered back to France, it became clear that forced immigration would be the only way to save John Law's enterprise. Male and female, the lowlife of Paris and the provinces were herded like animals into carts and drays, jammed into foul-smelling collection centers, crawling with vermin and disease. For the debauched regent, Philippe, soon to die of apoplectic seizure, it was a chance to scour the country of its human detritus. In June 1719, a group of 299 women was deported to Louisiana, accused by Paris police of an ''extraordinary degradation of habits.'' Sixteen women, aged 17 to 38, were branded with the *fleur de lis.* Some sadly contemptuous notations appear on the shipping list: ''Perfect Pig,'' ''Confirmed Debauchee,'' ''Knife Wielder,'' ''Accomplished in All Vices.''

They were chained by twos, piled into carts, and carried off to the wharves. Riots broke out. On one occasion, 150 women rebelled and mobbed a handful of guards. The frantic women kicked, bit, and scratched. Some attacked the gendarmes with their chains. Finally, the guards fired into the hysterical crowd. Six women were killed, perhaps 20 more wounded.

They died in camp, they died en route. They died where they landed, on

A Short History of New Orleans

the Gulf Coast. Half the cargo of these "pest flotillas" succumbed on some voyages. Conditions were often as horrible as on slave ships. It was inhuman, but efficient; it got the job done. Law's contract called for 6,000 settlers, and 3,000 slaves (the first 500 of whom arrived from Saint-Domingue in 1719, to be sold on credit). Between 1717 and 1721, his henchmen increased the population of Louisiana twenty times—from about 400 to 8,000. How many thousand died in the process, no one knows.

Father Charlevoix wrote that the *émigrés* were "miserable wretches driven from France for real or supposed crimes." They considered the new country "a place of exile," he said, and had no interest "in the progress of a colony of which they are only members in spite of themselves." Bienville was indignant. On October 20, 1719, he protested to the French government. "All I have is a band of deserters, smugglers, and scoundrels, who are ready not only to abandon you but also . . . to turn against you." It took a half-year to respond, but on May 9, 1720, the regent Philippe declared an end to the "deportation of criminals and undesirables to Louisiana."

By this time John Law was nearing the end of the line. In less than five years, the canny Scotsman had become the second most powerful man in France. He had reinforced his cozy alliance with Philippe by converting to Catholicism and was rewarded by being made Minister of Finance for the Empire. His propaganda had so inflamed jaded Parisians that, near the end, *Le Mississippi* stock was selling at 40 times its real value. One historian says wryly that John Law was about 200 years ahead of his time. His "credit-bank" was built on unlimited paper money, deficit financing—and inflation. And his pupil, the Duke of Orleans, helped sink him by operating a runaway printing press. When the bubble finally burst in October 1720, the national debt was 130 million livres, double what it had been when the Scotsman first outlined his scheme in a Paris gambling den.

John Law fled to England where he was vilified and scorned. He gambled away his few remaining years, wandering across Europe. When he died in Vienna in 1725, he was impoverished, as was France. Montesquieu observed: "The foreigner turned the state inside out, as a tailor turns a suit of clothes."

John Law and Philippe, Duke of Orleans (who died in 1723), almost bankrupted France, but together created one of the world's greatest cities. New Orleans was born of speculation and greed, a creature of chance and a child of fortune.

Bienville's Battle: The tiny hamlet on the Mississippi was under constant attack from the elements. The slightly elevated natural levee on which Bienville constructed the first flimsy hut was no match for the constant seepage, torrential rains, and gale winds that buffeted it in hurricane season. The huts were quickly swept away when the river overflowed, inundating the newly cleared streets. The ditches were filled to

The city that survived: A hurricane leveled its flimsy huts but New Orleans was rebuilt and looked like this in 1725. View is from site near today's Audubon Park.

From the beginning, New Orleans streets were bordered by drainage ditches and elevated *banquettes*. City blocks were called islets or islands, which, at times, they literally were.

overflowing, and each city square became its own island. By winter, the tiny refuge of his "beautiful crescent" served mainly as a stopover for parties going up river. The rich concessionaires, forbears of Louisiana's future cane planters, were hiring tenant farmers to till their bottom lands.

A certain Father Duval, in a letter to a Paris newspaper in 1719, wrote that "the town was one league around and composed of rustic houses, covered with immense pieces of bark and large reeds." Descriptions from visitors varied wildly, probably because wind and water continually blew the settlement down or washed it away. It flooded every year and 1719 was no exception. It was, the Indians said, the worst Big Water they had ever seen. The entire town was inundated.

For the first time, Bienville had doubts. The only defense against the river, he wrote, would be to build a levee system and dig a canal from the river to Lake Pontchartrain. That was to take about 75 years. His many critics and political opponents began to snipe at him again. Hubert, the commissary who vowed to make Natchez the capital, spoke of the mass exodus from New

Orleans to the town perched high on the bluffs. "There are in New Orleans," Hubert said, "but three Canadian houses and a store belonging to the Company."

For three years, New Orleans was virtually deserted, a depot for settlers and slaves headed for higher, drier land. The Company's engineers recommended a new spot be chosen. (With the collapse of John Law's papier-mâché empire, the Company was reorganized as the Company of the Indies.) Attempting to recoup their staggering losses and sagging prestige, the directors made Bienville their fall guy. A Company man was sent to expedite the phantom search for silver, gold, and those elusive pearl fisheries. The well-weathered Quebecois was now 42 and had spent more than half his years in Louisiana. Above all, he was a fighter. With the Company man otherwise engaged, Bienville finally convinced France to move the capital from Mobile to New Orleans. Magically all opposition melted away.

Bienville and a brilliant young engineer, Adrien de Pauger, immediately set about constructing a new city, beginning with a master plan. Their town would be laid out in the shape of a parallelogram, 4,000 feet long by 1,800 feet wide. It would be subdivided into 66 uniform squares, fronting on the river. Bienville reserved one large riverfront square as a parade ground, the Place d'Armes. Overlooking this square would be a church, a prison, a barracks, and a rectory. At last there would be permanence in his New Orleans, a renascent city that would defy anything man or nature might contrive to destroy its fragile setting.

The city planned by Pauger (now called The Vieux Carré) was conceived along Renaissance lines. It was held in shape by geography — the huge lake, the river and an encompassing swamp. This prevented urban sprawl, which has afflicted most American cities, and contributed to the old French city's urbanity and special charm.

The two men had no way of knowing how truly permanent their new city would be; its street plan is still in place today, one of the oldest in North America. The French Quarter is, in effect, a city within a city. The Place d'Armes, now Jackson Square, has become a striking signature for Bienville's persistent dream.

The new city's street-names fascinated Parisians. The main street was Royal, where the merchant princes would keep shop and live, as was the custom, upstairs. Bourbon Street was named for the royal family and, like it, was destined eventually for a fall from grace. Burgundy was a province in France. The royal bastards Conti and Toulouse were judiciously separated by St. Louis Street. And — the Company man having been recalled after finding no gold or pearls — Governor Bienville could begin building his new home — on Bienville Street.

New Orleans is fascinated by water. Streets have been named Basin, Levee, Canal, Water, Swamp, and Marais (morass or swamp). Any street within 10 blocks of the river was apt to be a *marais* and thus lost or *perdido* in Spanish. Naturally, New Orleans has a Perdido Street.

The first census, taken in November 1721, counted 470 people: 145 men, 65 women, 38 children, 29 white indentured servants, 172 Negro slaves, and 21 Indian slaves. There were also 36 cows and 9 horses. Three times as many people resided on the outskirts of the town, where ten times as many slaves

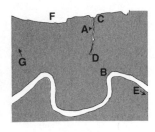

A. Bayou St. Jean
B. Original site (French Quarter)
C. Ft. St. Jean
D. Houmas Indian Village
E. To English Turn
F. Lake Pontchartrain
G. To Pass Manchac

worked the indigo plantations.

Bienville had imported the first two slaves from the West Indies in 1708. About the same time, the Commissary General, Martin d'Artaguette, began surveying the province for future needs. He recommended extensive use of slave labor as the only answer to the agricultural problem. D'Artaguette accurately predicted that French nobles, townsmen and artisans would shy away from physical labor and never toil in the fields. John Law's Company saw slaves as the only answer, even before large crops of cane or cotton became staple. Five thousand Africans were brought into the colony during a period of 10 years. Only 2,000 survived.

The Code Noir: In 1724, drawing upon a century of experience with "that peculiar institution" by both Spaniard and Frenchman in Saint-Domingue, Bienville promulgated the remarkable *Code Noir* (Black Code). The preamble banned Jews from the colony and prohibited Protestants from worship. Severe as the regulations and punishment were for blacks, the *Code Noir* was lenient compared to the harsh and dehumanizing practices followed by the English. The French insisted it was drawn up for the protection of their slaves. The Code forbade masters to work slaves on Sundays and required them to provide religious training. It honored slave families—up to a point—permitting marriages and forbidding sales that split the family unit. Slaves were permitted to own certain properties.

There was a perverse practicality in this. The French colonists soon found that their major investment was "human"; slaves performed better if guaranteed at least minimal human rights. Once slave labor developed from an institutional convenience into an economic necessity, these rules were increasingly overlooked or relaxed. By the time of the Civil War, there were perhaps 300,000 slaves in Louisiana.

With unwilling slave labor, Adrien de Pauger worked zealously to construct a permanent city in the hostile marsh, assisted by a former antagonist of Bienville's, Chief Engineer La Blond de la Tour. They lugged in cypress, the only wood that would stand up to New Orleans weather. The first raised cottages, so typical of the city, were elevated above the soggy ground. There were no rocks, not even pebbles. The oak-cypress delta had been built entirely of silt, sand, and clay. As work progressed and a new city began to take shape, the governor's confidence was slowly restored. He had survived three floods. An angry, restive populace periodically called for his hide. The Company used him as scapegoat. The nobles resented him. The politicians were jealous. Yet his city was being built on the "beautiful crescent" to his exact

The city's harsh environment inspired houses with wide porches or galleries overshadowed by a hipped roof making a breezeway. Tall doors, windows and ceilings promoted coolness. Louvered shutters protected against sun and rain. They were called *jalousies* (jealousies) because a lady could look out without being seen.

A Short History of New Orleans

specifications.

On September 11, 1722, the first hurricane officially recorded in Louisiana struck New Orleans. Fifteen hours later, 34 houses or huts had been destroyed, including the makeshift church and rectory. Ships laden with grain, fowl, and produce ran aground. An entire fleet of small vessels sank in the Mississippi. The river rose more than eight feet. Food was short and so was labor for rebuilding. The citizens were hostile. All their festering grievances boiled to the surface, and they wanted Bienville's head.

Bienville had ceded himself some river property four years before. It comprised a strip running eight miles along the riverfront on the city side and a generous tract on the west bank which today is Algiers. It was duly registered with John Law's Company, but the Crown later informed him the cession was not ethical. Told he could keep only enough for a "vegetable garden," the governor retained a plot about the size of today's downtown business district. Bienville eventually was allowed to recover his land and farm it. But the citizens kept carping, saying Bienville had saved the best riverfront lands for himself by pretending they were flooded lands and therefore worthless.

Other complaints from the settlers, the post commanders, and the petty officials were added to a lengthening list. He failed to provide food in Biloxi, they said, or replacements from France. His poor transportation system left thousands stranded on the beach. More than half the working men who had come to Biloxi died of hunger, disease, and lack of medical attention. For the Crown there was one overriding question—why hadn't the huge outlay of money produced any profit in five years?

A three-man secret investigatory council, led by Jacques de la Chaise, stole into New Orleans three months after the hurricane hit. It was disastrous to Bienville's career. On February 16, 1724, Bienville was stripped of his powers as Governor and recalled to France in dishonor.

When Bienville left New Orleans, he was banished from the city he founded and forbidden to return. France graciously awarded him an annual pension of 750 livres.

The German Coast: Mark Twain once said: "One might as well bully the comets in their courses . . . as try to bully the Mississippi into right and reasonable conduct." The natural levee formed by the Mississippi at New Orleans slopes gently into marsh; in places, the town is four to six feet below sea level. Repeated flooding finally convinced the colonists that they must develop a man-made levee system and some sort of drainage. The hurricane had proven that the little community was vulnerable not only to the rising water caused by river flooding, but to the deluge of rain brought by the 100-mile-an-hour winds of tropical storms.

Levee is French for "raised." Originally it was applied to a reception in the king's chambers.

The first major engineering project in New Orleans was the construction of artificial levees. The main levee, fronting the river, was one mile long, a yard high, and 18 feet wide at the top. But the derelicts John Law had conned or shanghaied had taken to gathering in Louisiana's squalid frontier towns to drink, gamble, and fight. The whole unproductive province was costing France a fortune it could ill afford. The major crops, indigo and tobacco, were inedible. To keep the colonists alive, food was shipped in from Illinois country, France, and the West Indies.

Before his bubble burst, Law sent his agents into Germany, where landless German peasants, victims of Louis XIV's ceaseless wars, eagerly reacted to inducements of land, farm animals, tools, and a one-year supply of food. At least 10,000 set out for Beulah land. They died like flies on pest flotillas, while others, weakened and unable to adapt to the southern climate, expired in Louisiana.

Those hardy Rhinelanders and tenacious Swiss who survived sought out John Law's personal concession in what is now Arkansas. Naturally, the Company failed to keep its promises. The Germans left their "Mournful Settlement" and drifted downriver on rafts and pirogues. Bienville invited them to make a home along the Mississippi, above New Orleans, on what is now called "The German Coast." The town of Des Allemands is a monument to their hegira. These Germans became the new colony's most productive, hard-working citizens. For generations, they worked the farms and dairies for New Orleans markets. They did not make the colony self-sufficient, but they markedly lessened the need for import. The Chevalier de Champigny described the German Coast as "the best cultivated, most thickly settled part of the colony" 50 years later.

Most of Louisiana's original German-given names were transmuted into French by French-speaking priests and officials who registered them. But the Germans stayed on, and in later years the aloof Creoles showed a grudging respect for them. Referring to any tough manual labor, they would say: "It takes German people to do that."

In marked contrast, New Orleans, the ragged settlement to the south of the German Coast, was already notorious for the loosest morals in the New World. At Biloxi Bay, Commander de Valdeterre complained: "The troops are without discipline, arms, or ammunition, most of the time without clothing, and they are frequently obliged to seek their food among the Indian tribes." In a bitter diatribe, he went on to bemoan "forgers, robbers, murderers . . . sure of immunity" and cases of arson, hijacking, and profiteering. "In short," he concluded, "this is a country which to the shame of France, be it said, is without religion, without discipline, without order, and without police."

A Short History of New Orleans

The first three deficiencies were remedied, to some extent, in August 1727, when a group of 12 Ursuline nuns established their first American colony in New Orleans. Bienville had requested an establishment of this highly respected order of teaching nuns, who specialize in the schooling of children and young women. He needed someone to administer the city's first hospital and orphanage, and to establish a girls' school.

The nuns would also chaperone the "*filles à la cassette*," the legendary "casket girls" who carried their dowries in small portable trunks. Unlike the British, whose wives helped them conquer the wilderness, French Louisiana suffered from a chronic shortage of women. Bienville had constantly exhorted the Company to "send me wives for my Canadians." He had received only hoydens. Ironically, the long-distance matchmaker was in exile when the casket girls arrived. They were mostly in their teens, middle-class, and educated, carrying all their belongings in lockers or small trunks, called *cassettes*. Each contained two dresses, two petticoats, six headdresses, and sundries.

A touch of grace: First the Ursuline nuns (left), then the "casket girls" carrying their dowries (right), softened the rude town's edges. The Ursuline Convent on Ursuline Avenue, completed in 1745, is the only surviving building from the French Colonial era, and the oldest structure in the Mississippi Valley.

They arrived to find New Orleans an irregular cluster of about 100 bark huts, a small church, some warehouses, and the governor's home. The ladies were locked up each night, under the watchful eye of the nuns. By day they promenaded through the city streets when the mud wasn't too deep, so the men could appraise them and make a choice. Within a few weeks, the French home office was informed, "This merchandise has been disposed of."

There were many remarkable women in the Ursuline order. One of these was Sister Xavier, the first woman pharmacist in America. She compounded medicines for the King's Hospital from a wondrous variety of plants and home-grown herbs. Lack of any proper medical care or medicines was, together with sanitation, the most grievous problem in the struggling town. The Ursulines specifically requested ample space for an herb garden.

For all its scruffiness, New Orleans was finally developing a culture. It began when the Ursulines and their casket girls disembarked and set about softening its wilderness heart. The population had almost doubled. Pauger's streets were named and new ones were being hacked out of the jungle. The local swamps were drained, and war had been declared on snakes, mosquitoes, and alligators.

New Orleans was still subject to food shortages and floods, and floating refuse made the open drains foul-smelling at times. But there was a hint of prosperity. Plantations lined the river from the Carrollton section of the city along the Tchoupitoulas coast to Cannes Brulées (Kenner). A crude roadway followed Bayou Metairie into Bayou St. John, where prosperous small farms had been settled. The staple crop was indigo, a purplish plant that yielded a strong bluish dye. Tobacco was being grown for the first time, and wax myrtle. (Cotton mills had been set up, but they proved inefficient at ginning.)

Sister Madeline, one impressionable Ursuline novice, wrote a letter home telling her family she found in New Orleans "as much magnificence and refinement as in France.... Our town is very handsome, well constructed, and regularly built, as much as I could judge on the day of our arrival.... The houses are well built ... the streets are large and straight ... the colonists are proud of their capital ... they sing a song on the streets ... that this town is as fine a sight as Paris."

Natchez Massacre: Historically, the French held onto their colonies by dealing with the Indians in an intelligent and diplomatic manner. They refrained from ridiculing Indian customs and beliefs. Always outnumbered by the affluent, standoffish British, Frenchmen mingled freely, trading and trapping, speaking the Indian language. They even sent their

None of Louisiana's first families admits descent from the girls of Saltpêtrière or the first shipment of hoydens. Herbert Asbury surmises that the genteel casket girls "must have been amazingly fertile and the earlier strumpets all barren."

Exports from the colony were negligible. The government promoted exotic industries such as wax making and silkworm farming. For years, the Ursulines taught young ladies to raise silkworms on the abundant mulberry leaves and weave the silk into dresses.

A Short History of New Orleans

sons out to live in Indian villages.

One of Bienville's greatest attributes had been his ability to deal fairly with the Indians. At some point, however, he became more intransigent. In pursuing a policy of reprisal, he stirred up one of the most uncontrollable passions of all, that mindless equivalent of Holy War the Indians called "blood vengeance."

In 1716 Bienville had built Fort Rosalie upstream among the warrior Natchez, and the fertile land attracted 300 settlers. This encroachment on Indian territory was not delicate, and a series of wars broke out. During the third Natchez war, Bienville burned their villages and demanded the head of the Sun Chief. His bloody tactics paved the way for a bloody uprising in 1729.

The man who set off the conflict was Captain Chepard, a Quebecois of towering incompetence, quite possibly insane. Chepard personally coveted a choice Indian plot near the fort. There he proposed to build his own plantation. The land was the sacred site of the Indians' burial ground and temple. When the bewildered Natchez asked two months' delay to harvest their crops, Chepard demanded a portion of their harvest, adding the indignity of extortion to the prospect of desecration. The embittered Natchez met in secret council with other tribes to plan a sneak attack. Only one tribe, the Choctaw, joined the conspiracy. Traditionally friends and allies of the French, the Choctaw agreed to attack New Orleans at the same time the Natchez surprised the French at Fort Rosalie.

The fatuous Chepard was repeatedly warned of such a possibility. He obstinately refused to believe those who contradicted his own misconceptions, and he put anyone in irons who even insinuated there might be a massacre. On the eve of the Natchez uprising, Chepard toured the Grand Village of the Indians, surveying the site of his future plantation. His retinue of servants and slaves came with him to prepare a great feast, which the commandant washed down with fine wine and brandy.

The next morning, a ceremonial party of Natchez arrived quite early at Fort Rosalie. In honor of Chepard and a royal guest, they announced a "grand hunt." They then scattered about the area, inside and outside the fort, ostensibly to purchase hunting rifles and ammunition, preparing their ambush. The Great Chief arrived next with his bravest warriors, laden with gifts and tribute for Chepard. Ironically, the Indians broke into their traditional dance of peace. Reaching crescendo, the peace dance abruptly stopped.

Screaming Indians appeared from everywhere and nowhere, firing rifles purchased from the French. They were inside the fort and concealed in French outposts throughout the area. The Fort Rosalie Natchez Massacre was over in minutes. The French were totally surprised, outnumbered, overwhelmed—and slaughtered. Estimates range from 300 to 700 killed, including those ambushed in the surrounding area. The Indians captured 150 children and 80 women to be sold as slaves. Chepard himself was deemed unworthy of death by the hands of noble warriors. The Sun Chief summoned the tribal grotesque, Little Snake, a misshapen cripple called the Stinkard. Little Snake gleefully clubbed Chepard to death with a wooden hatchet.

A storekeeper escaped and, with the help of friendly Indians, reached New Orleans. Bienville's successor, Governor Etienne de Perier, reacted with disbelief. He called for medical attention; the storekeeper was obviously hallucinating.

The Choctaw never did attack New Orleans. They became "confused" on the date agreed upon, thinking it was two days later. It is not clear whether the guileful Choctaw really intended to join the conspiracy. They may have planned to string along the Natchez, then leave them to suffer French wrath alone. Divided eternally by the swampy delta, the Choctaw had developed a predator's instinct for subterfuge. Or they may have simply been aggravated that the Natchez attacked early and took all the booty.

Following the Natchez Massacre, the nervous governor, Etienne de Perier, organized, reorganized, and disbanded black troops, then ordered a trench built around New Orleans. This dismal gutter was surmounted by a paling of sharp stakes, and lasted four years as the city's first and only line of defense.

A regiment of "dependable blacks" was formed in New Orleans for emergency action against the hostile natives. A black informant disclosed that some of the soldiers planned a "New Orleans massacre." The alleged conspirators were dealt with harshly. One woman was hanged and eight men tortured, then hanged.

It was whispered that the blacks and Indians were conspiring. The French moved to pit them against each other. Blacks were threatened with hanging "unless they proved their innocence" by attacking some Indians. Eighty blacks were given knives, hatchets, and bayonets, but not guns, and sent downriver to ambush a small Indian settlement of peaceful agrarians. Seven or eight innocent Indians were killed. This insidious stratagem irrevocably split the two races. Race relations, relatively benign until the Natchez Massacre, were never again the same in Louisiana. The carnage left the three races, whites, blacks, and Indians, malignantly suspicious of each other. Conspiracy was suspected everywhere.

Almost everyone in New Orleans lost a relative in the massacre. The Ursuline nuns were severely taxed in caring for the injured, the orphans, and the dislocated. Some blacks had been part of the conspiracy, and the Indians spared their lives only to sell them back into bondage. The Tunica Indians captured four Natchez braves and brought them to New Orleans. They were publicly burned alive in an elaborate civic ceremony by the levee. The Natchez retaliated, murdering the Tunica chief. Then, in an orgy of bloody recrimination, the Natchez destroyed the Tunica Nation.

Perier had set out to punish and destroy the Natchez Indians. The need of the colonists for their own "bloody vengeance" drove him to pursue the tribe all the way to north Louisiana, where the Sun Chief was captured and enslaved. Disease and attacks by other Indians gradually cut the proud Natchez to pieces. Some headed east and some took refuge with the Chickasaw.

In 1731, the Company of the Indies, John Law's legatees, turned back its license, having exhausted both its credit and its credibility. After six years of enforced exile, the founder, "Father" Bienville, once again was recruited to help his jittery city survive. New Orleans became a Crown Colony, and Bienville, who had already served three times as governor and had been discharged twice, was appointed for a final 12-year tour of duty. He promptly emancipated his two personal slaves and ceded his controversial eight miles of waterfront land to the Jesuits.

After being banished in 1763 and abolished by the Pope 10 years later, the Jesuits reorganized and returned to New Orleans in 1835. They established Loyola University in 1912.

But Bienville's last hurrah was a hollow one. The commander was determined to punish the Chickasaw for sheltering the Natchez. His allies, the enigmatic Choctaw, lined up with him, smiling; in the first battle, they broke and ran. During one siege, the Choctaw came forward to fire and stopped, 50 yards short of the firing line. Not only did their bullets fall short of the Chickasaw, but the Chickasaw fire fell safely short of the Choctaw. In another classic nonconfrontation, Bienville, thinking himself surrounded, sent a party out to sue for peace. The Chickasaw, believing they were surrounded, surrendered.

Bienville's own troops were routed in two major engagements and were finally driven back all the way to New Orleans. It was a short, inglorious campaign. Bienville, at 53, had grown testy and self-righteous. He bitterly complained of his troops' behavior, calling them "useless human beings," and insisted they were too short, some of them "only four-and-a-half feet tall."

Even with his "midget" army, the governor kept trying to punish the Chickasaw. He was forced to burn the fort he had built himself in 1716, Fort Rosalie, to forestall its capture by the enemy. Four years of campaigning cost France as much as Louisiana's entire budget. He would have done better to heed the old French maxim: "It often costs more to avenge injuries than to bear them."

Nobody, Indian, Spanish or French, ever conquered the Chickasaws. A small tribe, they moved west of the Mississippi in the 1820s and settled in Indian Territory (Oklahoma).

At 63, the founder was exhausted. France's profligate monarch, Louis XV, seemed more interested in spending public money on Madame Du Barry than on the colony. Bienville ended his fourth term as governor in 1743, after 41 years of service to Louisiana, and returned to France to live out his years as a country squire. When he left his city, his creation, New Orleans, he owned not an acre. His name adorned a Bayou (St. Jean) and a street in the Vieux

Carré. Yet his signature was everywhere. What, indeed, is a great life? "It is a dream of youth," said de Vigny, "found in old age."

Vaudreuil and Kerlerec: New Orleans' first "Golden Age" began in May 1743, when a stylish sophisticate from France arrived, Pierre-Cavagnal de Rigaud, Marquis de Vaudreuil. The Marquis set standards of corruption and frivolity unparalleled in the colonial outpost. He was determined to smooth away the frontier town's rough edges while instilling a sense of French courtliness, elegance, and *joie de vivre*. For 15 years, Vaudreuil and his wife presided over a little Versailles, a hedonistic round of balls, banquets, *fêtes*, card parties, and promenades. His state dinners were served on solid gold plates. His lavish entertainments captivated the colony, fatigued from threats of Indian and slave uprisings, hurricanes, and floods.

Some time during Vaudreuil's indulgent administration New Orleans began to celebrate Mardi Gras. The festival was deeply rooted in French custom, a pre-Lenten revelry that preceded 40 days of fasting. The first Carnival *bals masqués* (masked balls) were probably designed to spice up Vaudreuil's continual whirl of ordinary balls or soirées. A French officer visited New Orleans in 1743 and wrote: "Everyone here studies his own profit. The poor labor for a week, and squander in one day all they have earned in six; from thence arises the profit of the public houses, which flourish every day. The rich spend their time in . . . plays, balls, and feasts."

The first Mardi Gras street celebration was probably staged by a group called the Cowbellions, who raided a hardware store and roamed the streets jangling cowbells.

The Marquis and his elegant wife brought a shipload of magnificent furniture and trappings from France. He established his own provincial court and introduced theater to society. The first play produced in New Orleans, "The Indian Father," was performed in the governor's mansion in 1753. "The most common pastime," a French officer noted, "of the highest and lowest, and even the slaves, is women. Of the 500 women married, or unmarried, in New Orleans, I don't believe, without exaggeration, that there are ten of them of blameless character; as for me, I know but two of those, and even they are privately talked of."

New Orleans became a legend under Vaudreuil, renowned in London, Paris, and New York. Charity Hospital was rebuilt, organized corruption was reorganized, gambling was reinstated, and the first four-wheel carriage was imported from France. Both the city and Vaudreuil were greatly enriched. The Marquis apparently established an elaborate system of kickbacks and gouges. It was later charged he employed relatives in high posts, cut himself a percentage of all trade monopolies, and confiscated and sold Army provisions. He headed off investigation by conducting his own inquiry and then writing

St. John's Hospital for the Poor and Needy was America's first charity hospital. Burned down and blown down more than once, it is now a 1,200-bed colossus on Tulane Avenue.

A Short History of New Orleans

up an impressive list of new reform laws. Satisfied, he left for his new assignment as governor of Canada.

Vaudreuil, a nobleman, had been privileged to use his office for personal profit. His successor, Louis Billouart, Chevalier de Kerlerec, was not only base-born but an honest public servant—a rarity in France. He was probably the most able colonial governor after Bienville. But the Marquis having escaped untouched, Kerlerec was scapegoated for all his predecessor's shortcomings and then destroyed by the spying "commissaries."

France virtually abandoned New Orleans during the Seven Years' War. Kerlerec erected a fence four feet high around the city, ostensibly to guard against raiding Choctaws who had been introduced to the joys of scalping for profit by their new friends, the British. The fence also kept the slaves from running away. But it couldn't protect Kerlerec from his enemies within.

It is a bitter irony that few people remember Kerlerec except as the butt of a Choctaw joke. The Choctaw supposedly said Kerlerec never once told them the truth. So they, themselves no paragons of honor, named a body of water Chef Menteur (Chief Liar) after him. Kerlerec was recalled to France in 1763 and thrown into the Bastille. He was charged with "mismanaging" a colony which had not seen a French ship in four years and had already, secretly, been traded away to Spain.

Somebody had to take the blame.

French government traditionally operated *bon plaisir* (at the King's pleasure). Almost every office was bought and was expected to yield a fat profit. Joe Gray Taylor says: "Probably the origin of chronic corruption in Louisiana government can be traced to the French attitude that public office was a form of property from which the holder should profit."

The Spanish Years

3

It struck like a lightning bolt cleaving a cloudless sky. In October 1764 Jean Jacques Blaise d'Abbadie, the newly appointed Director General of New Orleans, announced to his French-speaking citizenry that they were all subjects of the Spanish king.

To compound their misery (and shock) they discovered a "secret" which had been kept from them for two years! Inconceivable as it was, the derelict King Louis XV had presented the Isle of Orleans and most of Louisiana province to his first cousin once removed, Charles III of Spain, at Fontainebleau, on November 13, 1762.

Spain had entered the Seven Years' War belatedly, honoring a Bourbon "Family Compact." New Orleans was compensation for Spain's having lost Manila and Havana as well as Florida. For his part, Louis was delighted to unload the unproductive Louisiana province and New Orleans. It was costing one and a half million dollars a year to support.

The armed conflict had begun as the French and Indian War in the backwoods of Pennsylvania. A young British officer named George Washington attacked Fort Duquesne (now Pittsburgh) and defeated the French in the first battle. It spread to Europe and eventually became a world war. It devastated the French Empire. A British army stormed the Plains of Abraham and took Quebec in 1759. Montreal fell in 1760.

New Orleans was completely cut off and orphaned from the French world of its forefathers. In four years, its citizens warranted only one visit; three French ships arrived April 29, 1762, carrying troops, dispatches, and some food.

When the treaty of Paris was signed on February 10, 1763, Great Britain received Canada and all French possessions east of the river, including Baton

"The Family Compact" was dreamed up by Louis XIV when he ensconced his great-grandson on the throne of Spain as Charles III. His grandson and heir, Louis XV, employed the compact to entice cousin Charles into the disastrous Seven Years War.

Opposite page
Corridor of time: The New Orleans patio (here, off Royal Street) is a reminder of the "French Quarter's" Spanish heritage.

Rouge, Natchez, and Mobile. The Spanish Floridas also went to the British. Spain received all French land west of the Mississippi and, by secret covenant, the Isle of Orleans. The French Empire in North America was reduced to two small unfortified islands south of Newfoundland, Saint Pierre and Miquelon. Spain became England's sole remaining rival in North America.

"The news threw the colony into consternation and despair," wrote historian Alcée Fortier. New Orleans had been "abandoned to an unknown ruler." The country surrounding New Orleans was given away. The British now enjoyed free passage the length of the river and were setting up "floating warehouses." Having learned amity from the French, the British wooed the Southeastern Indians with gifts. Soon the Indians held their first convention, a great congress of nations, attended by 3,000 natives, near Mobile. The Choctaws had grown sullen. Their former French allies had reneged on their promises. The British were quick to capitalize on their anger.

New Orleans was tense for other reasons. A revolt in Saint-Domingue had caused Governor Kerlerec to ban all slave importation from the West Indies. Runaways were punished severely with floggings, brandings, and executions. Death was the penalty when animals were killed or stolen, a food shortage having made loss of livestock a peril. Whites lived in constant dread of a black revolt. A slave named Ceaser was tortured to solve a series of thefts—a chicken, a pig, clothes on a line. His execution was agonizingly brutal. Slave Ceaser was whipped, branded on the cheek, and his wrists were cut. Then he was broken on the rack.

In New Orleans, seven of every ten citizens were bankrupt. Seeking trade outlets, d'Abbadie encouraged illegal bartering with the British and open smuggling of slaves. Slave trade routes through Barataria, Lake Borgne, and the bayous were so busy that smuggling represented 20 percent of the colony's total trade by 1765.

The gentle, hard-working Director General experienced strange feelings of dizziness in the winter of 1764. He kept a journal until his arms were paralyzed. Some said he had yellow fever. Others rumored it was lead poisoning. Jean Jacques d'Abbadie died on February 4, 1765. Months passed and still no Spanish officials arrived. Citizens were bewildered and growing angry. Some feared French-issued money would become worthless. But the French flag still flew over New Orleans.

Jean Milhet, the richest merchant in the colony, was dispatched to France in hopes of persuading Louis XV to take his orphaned city back. Some historians say Milhet sought out the aging Bienville, a tottering 82-year-old man with "wild white hair." The King, though, was preoccupied. He had just abolished Parliament and sent its members home. Now he was putting together a more compliant legislature. The treasury was bare, in part because of the 20 million livres a year Madame Du Barry reportedly required to sate her stupendous appetites. Louis was too busy to see the Orleanians.

While Spain procrastinated, fate thrust two reasonable and moderate men into its crucible, Captain Charles Philippe Aubry, the ranking officer with the dubious task of serving two sovereigns, and Don Antonio de Ulloa, Spain's first Governor. Ulloa was one of Europe's leading scholars, a scientist and author, 50 years of age, a brilliant intellectual with no administrative experience. He came to govern compassionately—his instructions were that no change in local government be made.

A terrible storm crashed down on the city the night Ulloa disembarked, accompanied by 80 men, "enough to antagonize but not control." The Spaniards brought with them Catalonian wine in casks, a beverage offensive to those weaned on Bordeaux. Almost everything else the Iberian scholar did was even more ill-considered. He reduced the 35-livre salaries of his own men to the same pitiful seven livres the ragtag local soldiers received. Many of his men quit, and the Frenchmen refused to re-enlist.

Ulloa: The shy, mild-mannered scholar kept to himself most of the time. Then after six months' residence he came out of seclusion to issue his first decree. It effectively limited sales and currency so much that the city's large volume of contraband and speculative enterprise, including smuggling slaves, would be eliminated. With this he left a bewildered Aubry to run the city and sailed down the river, anchoring at Balise. No one knew why. Later, citizens heard that their enigmatic governor was building a barracks, and they were truly perplexed.

A spirit of insurrection quietly smouldered in New Orleans. It was kindled in part by the new Spanish regulation prohibiting importation of any wines except those produced in Spain. Ulloa waited seven months at the river's end. He finally returned from Balise with a bride. A Peruvian heiress, she arrived in grand style, leading a small army of servants and friends.

The city's Creole women, eager to inspect the Andean beauty, hastened to Ulloa's home to "call." The lady refused to see them. Doña Ulloa compounded the slight; she held parties, suppers and balls to which the local French were not invited. That was the unkindest cut—the "direct cut," the French Creoles call it. French gallants converged on the city from nearby plantations, villages, and farms. Attorney General Nicolas Chauvin La Frenière spoke passionately, and a petition demanding Ulloa's recall was signed by 560 citizens. On the night of October 27, the guns at the gates of

Charles Philippe Aubry, interim officer while New Orleans anxiously awaited Spanish rule, was maligned by Creole patriots for saying, "I command for the King of France and at the same time I govern as if it belonged to the King of Spain."

New Orleans were spiked.

The next day some 400 Orleanians, led by local merchants, raised hell in the Square. Some were drinking heavily. They demanded "the wine of Bordeaux, not the poison of Catalonia." It was a mock-serious display, six years of pent-up anxieties and outrage being vented on the Iberian scholar and his snobbish wife.

The protesters were also outraged that one of Ulloa's officers had married a dark-skinned Indian girl from Peru. The embittered Creole women denounced the union as illegal race-mixing, a violation of the *Code Noir*. Ulloa, fearing for his family's safety, took refuge on a ship anchored in the river. The Director General begged his people to be reasonable and avoid any incident. But that night, a group of revelers returning from a wedding decided to have some sport. Fortified with drink young Joseph Petit swam out and cut the ship adrift. Ulloa ended up on a sandbar. This was one insult too many. The enraged governor and his bride sailed the next day for Havana.

Creole historians have romanticized the insurrection, comparing it generously to the American Revolution. Joe Gray Taylor concedes some resemblances, but insists there is little indication the rebels had any plan at all. Actually, the Insurrection of October 27, 1768, probably arose from basic economic grievances. Ulloa's edicts banning illicit trade threatened the income of the ringleader, Attorney General La Frenière, and others. Illegal trading was a prime source of their wealth, French paper money was being recalled, and little Spanish lucre had replaced it. Colonists also must have feared that their exports—lumber, indigo, fur, tobacco, cotton, and sugar—would not have a market in Spain.

There was desperate talk after the insurrection of setting up a Republic in Louisiana. The conspirators made a futile appeal to the British governor of West Florida. He was obviously not interested in encouraging colonial revolts. A colony of 12,000, half of them slaves, stood little chance against the might of Spain. In Taylor's words, "it would be as if Georgia alone had rebelled against British rule in 1775."

For almost a year, Aubry presided over a populace that began to believe its own fantasies, including the exhilarating notion that it had successfully defied Charles III. Angered by the uprising, Charles summoned a Great Council to Madrid. For three months it debated what to do about the upstart colony. Spain saw Louisiana as a strategic buffer against England and viewed the revolt as one likely to provoke other colonial rebellions unless it were repressed.

Finally the King called in his favorite troubleshooter, dashing Don Alejandro O'Reilly. An Irish-born soldier of fortune, O'Reilly had fled English

In New Orleans, a Creole is a native-born Orleanian of French and/or Spanish extraction. The word comes from the Spanish *criollo*—a child born in the colony. Creole is also an attitude or type: Creole cuisine, Creole music, Creole customs, Creole tomatoes (extra large), and Creole cream cheese (impossible to describe).

persecution of Catholics, and had served various sovereigns before entering the Spanish army. In 1765 he saved King Charles's life during a riot in Madrid. O'Reilly was instructed to punish the New Orleans ringleaders. In 1769 he set sail with an armada of 24 ships, 2,000 men, and 50 cannon.

On July 26 Governor Aubry announced the arrival of a Spanish fleet at Balise. The following day, the Spanish marched into New Orleans to the sound of bugles and drums, cannon salvos, and small arms fire. In the Plaza de Armas, General Alejandro O'Reilly proclaimed that French *Louisiane* was now and truly Spanish *Luisiana*.

O'Reilly wasted little time dispelling any notion that the rebels would escape punishment. He summoned Aubry to his office and ordered the Frenchman to give him a list of the revolutionary leaders. Then he invited all 12 to a reception, called them aside, and arrested them.

Creole historians have bitterly condemned both Aubry and O'Reilly. But Aubry had repeatedly warned the ringleaders they could not defy Spain and escape the consequences. And O'Reilly, a military man, was under orders. La Frenière and four others went before a firing squad; another condemned man had died in prison. Six conspirators were imprisoned but released within a year. Amnesty was granted to all participants in the rebellion other than the leaders. New Orleans citizens then were ordered to pledge allegiance to the King of Spain.

"Bloody" O'Reilly: This Irish expatriate in Spanish service executed seven French patriots. Creole historians haven't forgiven him.

The Irish Spaniard: The new Spanish governor inevitably went down in Creole history as a tyrant, "Bloody O'Reilly," villain of America's first colonial revolution. Other historians have been kinder, and more objective. They feel that had O'Reilly acted differently he would have encouraged further rebellion. The hated O'Reilly stayed for only seven months, but he was a whirlwind of purposeful activity. A forceful administrator, he gave form and substance to the new government, while respecting French customs. First, O'Reilly ordered a long overdue New Orleans census. It showed 3,190 persons of all ages, sexes, and colors. There were 1,225 Negro slaves, and already 100 free people of color or *gens de couleur libre*. The Irishman and his census-takers toured the new Spanish province of Luisiana and determined that it had 13,538 residents, fully half of whom were slaves.

O'Reilly was quick to grasp the economic significance of these black chattels. In changing from French law to Spanish, he abrogated all existing French statutes with the exception of Bienville's *Code Noir*. It would appear that slavery so rapidly became essential that it came to be viewed as dispassionately as the internal combustion engine is in our own century. But the

Alejandro O'Reilly was one of several Irish exiles who found favor with the Spanish King. Ambrosio O'Higgins served Spain as Viceroy of Peru. His son, Bernardo O'Higgins, was a Chilean revolutionary hero who rivals Bolivar and San Martin in the affections of Latin Americans.

"lenient," romanticized *Code Noir* was honored more in the breach than in the observance. A Frenchman, C. C. Robin, who toured the province extensively, indicted the Creoles as inhumane hypocrites and said they held the "idea that the Negro is only a property which they dispose of at their pleasure." Slave-masters, he charged, generally "disregarded the laws designed to protect the blacks." In the end, Creoles apparently believed that "the abasement of the colored people" was essential to preserve slavery.

Alejandro O'Reilly abolished the old French Superior Council and replaced it with the Cabildo, or town council. Its six councilmen, or *regidores*, bought their offices for life, subject to periodic rebidding. Both Spanish and French government were based on the time-honored principle that "public office was personal property," to be used for private gain and, wherever possible, sold, auctioned, or bartered. Although neither the Spanish nor the French considered such practices corrupt, the Frenchman Robin appeared to be appalled. Corruption, he wrote, "makes frightful ravages here in disregard of the law." As one example, he mentioned Don Andrés Almonester, who arrived as a poor man, amassed "the richest fortune in the country and became New Orleans' leading philanthropist, having achieved his great wealth through the shadowy paths of corruption." Historian Jo Ann Corrigan maintains that corruption in Louisiana was not a Spanish innovation: "It was the one French tradition most easily adapted to Spanish ways." The Spanish legal code actually contained a list of fees charged for "personal" public services. This legacy of legitimized graft is deeply rooted in Louisiana politics even today. One observer has said that Louisianans "look upon the public as sheep to be shorn, and *office* as the special fleece."

In his seven short months O'Reilly also initiated Louisiana's first revenue tax, levied on places of amusement—taverns, inns, hotels, and cafes. But his most far-sighted policy granted any and all settlers, regardless of nationality, a plot of land, provided they could ably farm. He thus increased production in his Spanish domain.

The Promised Land: They were "scattered like snowflakes," Longfellow said. In 1755, 7,000 French Canadians who refused to swear allegiance to Great Britain were deported by the British from their homeland in Acadia (Nova Scotia) with little more than the clothes on their backs. It seemed doubly cruel since the British were the latecomers to that peninsula, arriving long after the first Acadians settled in 1605. Houses and barns were burned and, with little notice, the exiles were dumped on unsuspecting port cities up and down the Atlantic seaboard. Many served as inden-

It is amazing how observers differed when confronted by slavery. In 1776 Bouligny wrote: "The Negroes are slaves only in name, for in reality they are as happy as laborers may be in Europe." Robin disagreed: "Creoles deal with slaves as playthings of their whims."

Grand dérangement: Cruelly exiled from Nova Scotia, the Acadians (Cajuns) found their *terre bonne* in Louisiana.

A Short History of New Orleans

tured servants for wealthy families in New York and Philadelphia. Some wandered back to Acadia and were thrown out again. Others were lost at sea or died of malnutrition or sickness. Many returned to France.

The migration of the Acadians, or Cajuns, has been largely ignored by American historians. The Spanish authorities in Louisiana were enthusiastic about these hardworking agrarians. Louisiana faced a very palpable food shortage, and the Spaniards offered very palpable inducements: free land, seeds, tools, livestock, and often transportation. In 1769, a large Cajun contingent arrived from Baltimore. Simple farming people of purest French extraction from the coastal regions of Normandy, Brittany, and Acadia, they moved out into the bayous and prairie land.

According to the historian Joe Gray Taylor, the Acadian migration was the largest mass movement of ethnic immigrants in American colonial history. Thirty years after the *grand dérangement* by the British in Nova Scotia, over 5,000 Acadians had settled in Louisiana. (Today the Cajuns number more than 500,000, a prolific, healthy, family-oriented people.) The Spanish *intendante* in New Orleans, Martín Navarro, extolled their "enthusiasm, industry, and loyalty." He accurately predicted that they would greatly "increase the prosperity of our province." After half a century, colonial Louisiana had finally found Frenchmen willing to till the soil.

The Spaniards governed the colony for only 34 years. Their influence was mainly administrative and architectural. Very few Spanish settlers arrived. A group of Canary Islanders (or *Isleños*) followed Bernardo de Gálvez, later governor of the province. They settled below the city in what is now St. Bernard Parish, and their descendants there still trap, hunt, and fish. Another contingent, from Málaga, discovered the lower Teche, a long, navigable bayou leading to the Gulf. Here was established the only purely Spanish city of colonial times, New Iberia. Strangely enough, the supposedly intolerant *regidores* allowed freedom of conscience to Protestant immigrants, although they were forbidden to worship in public. In the 1770s groups of immigrants from the British colonies arrived; after 1779, more came from the fledgling United States. The Americanization of New Orleans had begun. The first rumblings, however, were distantly heard in the year 1769, when the British took over the eastern half of the continent and drove out the French. The Spanish controlled the southwest, and the Indians were temporarily allowed to roam with the buffalo, somewhere in between.

Even as O'Reilly tidied up and prepared to leave, ominous messages came down from the northeast. British citizens were refusing to pay the Stamp Tax or the despised Townshend duties on imports. The same colonists were also grousing over a tax on tea. The colonial city of New Orleans still

The Cajuns of Nova Scotia (Acadia) came from the northern French coast, Brittany, Normandy, and Picardy. The name Acadia is derived from the title of a 15th-century pastoral poem, "Arcadia" (the enchanted land).

Cajuns have retained their own language for two centuries. They insist it is the King's French spoken by 17th-century explorers Bienville and La Salle.

grumbled over Spanish "occupation," but its new overlords at least spoke a civilized romance language and liked their food spicy and their public officials flexible. O'Reilly had imposed order on the prodigal city, but he refused to play despot. French Creoles were admitted to high office; they retained their language and customs.

Pollock and Gálvez: The pressures of feeding an army, 2,000 extra mouths, had created a serious food shortage in New Orleans. A practical man, O'Reilly winked at his own shipping rules and allowed British ships to anchor in midstream and bring their goods ashore in lighters. One of the British merchants was a fellow Irishman out of Philadelphia whose loyalties were shaky. His name was Oliver Pollock.

Pollock endeared himself for life to Alejandro O'Reilly by turning over an entire shipload of flour, for whatever the governor chose to pay. The governor reciprocated by giving Pollock unlimited trading rights. Within ten years, he was a millionaire. Meanwhile, O'Reilly expelled the other five British merchants in port. After all, the king had instructed him to halt all illegal trade.

Oliver Pollock was destined to become a hero of the American Revolution. Born in northern Ireland and reared in Pennsylvania, he had joined a large mercantile company. In Havana, he first met O'Reilly, who shared his Irishman's contempt for the British. O'Reilly was called back to Spain in 1770, the year of the Boston Massacre. Oliver Pollock stayed in New Orleans. He bought a house on Chartres Street and married an Irish lass named Margaret O'Brien. Somewhere along the line he became a Spanish army liaison and an American Revolutionary agent.

Spain was of two minds about the threatened American rebellion. King Charles could hardly encourage colonists of another nation to defy their sovereign. Yet the British threatened Spain at Pensacola, Baton Rouge, Manchac, and Natchez. And Spain still rankled over the loss of Manila and the Floridas. In one of the surreptitious undercover deals that ornament colonial history, Spain retrieved Manila, but the British still controlled Caribbean shipping and Spanish commerce. It was decided that if and when Spain went to war, she would fight as France's *ally*, not *with* the United States.

Bernardo de Gálvez became Louisiana's governor in 1777, the year American patriots captured 7,000 British at Saratoga, bringing France into the fight. Pollock had already cast his lot, endorsing $10,000 worth of provisions for shipment upriver to defend what is now Pittsburgh and Wheeling. In a brilliant display of long-distance financing and covert trans-shipping, Pollock

Irishmen like Pollock and O'Reilly shaped the history of New Orleans long before the Anglos arrived. The first St. Patrick's Day celebration was held in 1806, six years before Louisiana achieved statehood.

channeled tens of thousands of dollars in supplies to the frontier fighter George Rogers Clark. During the summer of 1778, Clark swept across the northern Ohio Valley into Illinois country, the "American Bottom," and captured Kaskaskia, Cahokia, and Vincennes. Pollock's supplies, ammunition, gunpowder, and unlimited credit supported him, and French settlers, bitterly antagonistic to the British, rose to help the revolutionary.

Spain went to war on June 1, 1779, careful to explain that it was an ally of France. In New Orleans, Bernardo de Gálvez' aide-de-camp was Oliver Pollock. Gálvez was only 31 years old when he took command with orders to capture West Florida. His city was defenseless, guarded only by its natural fortifications, the lake, river, and swamp. He knew only one military technique—attack. Gálvez must have grimaced when he reviewed his troops. There were 600 men, of whom 450 were raw recruits. Most of them were disabled by sickness and fever. The pessimistic Cabildo, unaware of his orders to march on Florida, recommended that Gálvez surrender immediately if attacked.

The Spanish called Gálvez' bold campaign "The Glorious March." It began on August 18, 1779, and it almost ended before it started. A hurricane smashed New Orleans and sank his boats. Gálvez regrouped, and his army picked up spirit, and reinforcements, as they headed for Baton Rouge. The nominally Spanish army was a splendid cross-section of emerging America: Spanish, French, some Acadians, a number of Germans, 80 free men of color, and 60 Indians. There were seven Americans, including Oliver Pollock, representing the Continental Congress. By the time it reached Baton Rouge this war-whooping foreign legion was 1,400 strong, with three gunboats and one schooner.

For six weeks, the British had toiled to erect fortifications at Baton Rouge. They mustered 400 regular troops, 150 settlers and armed blacks, and 13 cannon. Gálvez drove his men so hard that many of them collapsed. But when the artillery sounded the morning of September 21, Gálvez' International Brigade was ready. By mid-afternoon the British surrendered.

By the terms of the British capitulation, Natchez was also made to surrender. Manchac already had fallen with little resistance. The boy general had effectively "cleared" the Mississippi River as far as St. Louis of all British obstacles.

Gálvez next set his sights on Mobile and Pensacola, intent on removing all British threats to Spain's Caribbean trade route. He mustered 1,000 men and tried to enter Mobile Bay with commandeered ships. A tropical storm turned the tranquil bay into a maelstrom. Several ships went aground. Many men and guns were lost. But within a month, he sneaked back and put

Pollock's money helped George Rogers Clark secure the "Old Northwest" (today's Midwest) for the United States. Like Pollock, Clark was penniless at war's end.

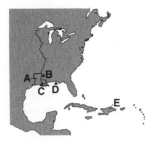

A. Present-day Louisiana
B. Natchez
C. Baton Rouge
D. Pensacola
E. Saint-Domingue
   (Hispaniola)

Mobile under siege. Twelve days later, the British surrendered. Gálvez had outrun the clock again; 1,000 British troops were less than 50 miles away. They had come by forced march from Pensacola hoping to lift the siege.

In 1780, Gálvez set sail for Pensacola with 4,000 men only to have his fleet scattered by hurricane winds.

Eight months later, the indomitable Gálvez returned, boldly ran the British guns guarding the harbor, and laid siege to Pensacola. Somehow, he had mustered 7,000 men from New Orleans, Mobile, and Havana. For two and one-half months his artillery pounded away at the British garrison of 2,600 troops, many of whom were Indians. A lucky hit on the powder magazine finally led to Pensacola's surrender on May 10, 1781. Bernardo de Gálvez' Glorious March had swept the Floridas clean, gained control of the Mississippi, and hastened the triumph of America's Revolution.

Further north, Lord Charles Cornwallis sought desperately to avoid entrapment in North Carolina. It mattered little, for Cornwallis was on the way to his fateful rendezvous at Yorktown in October 1781. There, while a British band played "The World Turned Upside Down," 8,000 British troops laid down their arms. With the British defeated, Spain regained the Floridas, and Great Britain was left with Canada as its sole possession in North America. The war crushed France financially. Staggering debts incurred during six years of fighting helped to bring on bankruptcy and the "deluge," the French Revolution.

Ironically, by aiding the revolution the Spanish had helped create a strong new enemy. The aggressive infant American nation was naturally expansionist and daring. It posed a greater threat to Spanish control of Louisiana and the Floridas than France or England ever did. In fact, within 40 years, all that Spain had gained would be Americanized, including New Orleans.

After the war, young Gálvez married a French girl and became the most popular man in the colony, the first genuine Creole folk hero. Spain lavished honors and titles on him; he was Viceroy of New Spain with control over Cuba and Louisiana. He seemed impelled by his youth to court danger, "the spur of great minds," remembering perhaps that it also was "the inseparable companion of honor."

At the age of 38, the "chivalric" Gálvez at least in one respect equalled his illustrious father, who had been Viceroy of Mexico. He, too, was elevated to that high office. Eight years later, the conqueror of Baton Rouge, Mobile, and Pensacola was dead. He was 46 years old.

Louisiana's other revolutionary hero, Oliver Pollock, lived to be 95. The fourth largest financier of the Revolution, he had sacrificed his entire fortune on the way to Yorktown. His support of George Rogers Clark had stretched the American boundaries from the Alleghenies to the Mississippi. But Pollock was thrown into debtors' prison after the war. The resourceful Irishman paid his lawyer $1,760 to keep the cell warm while he went out, paid off his debts, and built another fortune.

To help finance the revolution, Pollock mortgaged his property, put his slaves to work on public lands to cover loans, and borrowed money from the Spanish treasury as well as friends.

The Great Fires: In 1788, after 20 years of Spanish possession, the population of Louisiana had tripled, amounting to 42,346, including 18,000 slaves. New Orleans, with 5,338 residents, had doubled in size, but it was still a dirty port town, dominated by crude wooden cabins and infested with reptiles and insects that bred profusely in the surrounding swamp. One attempt to build a two-storied barracks failed when the baseboards rotted and the whole structure began to sink.

On March 21, a Good Friday, a lighted candle in the private chapel of Don Vincente José Nuñez quietly fell onto the lace curtains at his home on Chartres Street. A brisk south wind spread the flames so rapidly that the entire Vieux Carré was an inferno within an hour. The fire raged out of control for five hours, destroying 856 buildings. The church, the Cabildo, the prison, the arsenal, the government building, the Capuchin monastery, and most of the residences were leveled.

The mythology that surrounds this Good Friday holocaust has it that the Capuchins courted disaster by refusing to ring the church bells, the usual warning to fire volunteers; the bells were muffled for Holy Friday in ritual mourning of the Saviour's death. There is doubt that anyone could have averted the catastrophe, however. New Orleans' wooden buildings were tinder. The city's volunteer firemen were so poorly equipped that the best they could do was form a plodding bucket brigade up from the river.

Don Esteban de Miro, the new governor, reported a staggering $2½ million in losses and moved quickly to provide emergency shelter and food. "By a miracle," its records proclaim, the Ursuline convent was spared. Set far back from the street in its walled garden, the convent was built of brick and tile.

Six years later, on December 8, 1794, another fire broke out. According to some accounts, it began in a courtyard on Royal Street where children were playing next to a hayloft. A busy wind whipped the flames across the city, burning 212 buildings and all but two stores in the business section. From Canal Street to Orleans, from the river to Bourbon Street, 40 city blocks were erased.

The fifth, and probably the most skilled, governor of the Spanish period was a native of Flanders in the service of Spain. Don Francisco Luis Hector, Baron de Carondelet, faced the challenge of building almost a completely new city. Carondelet reported that, although fewer houses were razed, the monetary loss was greater than that from the conflagration of 1788. If such calamity can be called fortunate, this blaze was a peculiar blessing. Historian Grace King explains: "What lay in the ashes was at best, but an irregular, ill-built French town . . . what arose from them was a stately Spanish city, proportioned with grace and built with solidity."

The result was the oddly misnamed French Quarter, built almost entirely in the old Spanish style, the romantic city-within-a-city that still enchants visitors from around the world. Of the old French town, only the Ursuline convent survived.

Almonester: During the last decade of Spanish rule, the present Presbytère and Cabildo were built, flanking the Cathedral on the Plaza de Armas, now Jackson Square. The Cathedral was financed by a legendary man with the imposing name of Don Andrés Almonester y Roxas. He was the richest man in the colony and, according to more than one romantic historian, the most philanthropic. "Standing amid the smouldering ruins of the city," Lyle Saxon relates, "he pledged to build a church for the colony, rebuild the hospital, and to erect a new Cabildo, and a monastery for the Capuchins."

Don Andrés arrived in New Orleans with Alejandro O'Reilly in 1769. He was 44 years of age and mourning the death of his wife and child. He made a stunning debut at the Cabildo, laying before the *regidores* a series of documents, signed by King Charles, appointing Almonester Royal Clerk, Royal Notary, and Captain of the Louisiana Militia. Don Andrés then quietly went about acquiring the sites, lot by lot, of today's magnificent Pontalba buildings, flanking the Plaza de Armas. He became very rich very quickly.

Almonester built a row of rental houses and a mansion for himself on the square. Soon he had a plantation upriver with 100 slaves. The great fire of 1788 spared his houses while leaving most people homeless. Almonester promptly raised his rents. His tenants protested, but Almonester went ahead and promptly raised his rents.

In his book *Saint or Scoundrel?*, Jack Holmes traces the "shadowy paths" Don Andrés trod to become wealthy. By political arrangement, he finagled the job of notary for the city, the army, and the treasury. He served as official witness in court and as notary-attorney for every case involving property.

As Holmes describes it, "Almonester was able to learn, through his offi-

Spanish architecture was, by virtue of its evolution in Mexico and Puerto Rico, ideally suited for New Orleans. The Seignoret house at 520 Royal is a fine example of the style.

The Presbytère, begun in 1794, was completed by the Americans in 1813. The Cabildo, seat of Spanish government, was rebuilt in 1795 following the second great fire. The official transfer of Louisiana to the United States took place on the second floor in 1803.

cial post, of sales of land and slaves and to enter low bids for valuable property.'' He was, strangely enough, never underbid on anything, and made a fortune in real estate speculation and the construction business. He also contracted for the supply of labor and materials.

It's no wonder that Don Andrés' halo is slightly tarnished today, for his "philanthropies" invariably involved constructing something requiring lots of labor and materials. He built an isolation ward for lepers outside town. When a hurricane damaged the Charity Hospital, he paid for repairs. In 1787, he built a chapel and gave it to the Ursuline nuns. In 1788, following the first inferno, he rebuilt St. Louis Cathedral at his own expense and then put up funds to build the Cabildo and Presbytère. He was so rich he lent money to the town council.

Don Andrés was architect, contractor, supplier, and subcontractor for labor and supplies on all of his monuments. He did, though, donate perhaps $500,000 in labor, material, and services. From his plantation works he provided bricks, lime, and timber. He purchased raw iron for his blacksmiths and locksmiths. He deployed 100 slaves from his own fields. All this he volunteered, along with his own bricklayers, masons, joiners, carpenters, and helpers.

Don Andrés was not only the richest man in town, he married wealth in a June-November Creole wedding. Almonester was 60 years old. His bride was 29-year-old Louise de la Ronde, the daughter of an eccentric French plantation owner whose mansion, Versailles, was a purported replica of Louis XIV's palace. When Almonester was 70 a daughter was born: Micaela Almonester. She was destined to redesign the Plaza de Armas, running the whole show in jodhpurs, tongue-lashing contractors, overseeing every detail, just like Papa.

Almonester's construction team was busy preparing a new arsenal, a new calaboose, and the first French Market when the saintly scoundrel passed away in 1798. Controversy pursued him even to the grave. Years later, New Orleans named a street after him—and misspelled Almonester as Almonaster.

A stately Spanish city rose from the ashes of the fire of 1794. The new city was built to stand the ravages of wind, weather, and fire, a brick and plaster city, with proud arches of heavy masonry and roofs of Spanish tile. Long, deep-shadowed corridors, or *portes cochères*, entered onto patios splashed with the color of wild banana trees, sweet oleander, and other tropical plants. The houses were two-storied, the shop below, the residence upstairs. They hugged the banquettes (or sidewalks) and were surmounted by cool galleries, or balconies, ornamented decorously with hand-crafted filigreed wrought iron: an equipoise of delicate artistry and commanding strength.

Almonester's young widow soon remarried a young man seven years her junior. Indignant citizens turned out for a three-day charivari. They carried her dead husband's effigy and refused to leave until she donated $3,000 for an outdoor mass.

The Kaintocks: American flatboatmen poured down the river, drinking and brawling, threatening to invade New Orleans — until Jefferson purchased it and half the West.

The city's scale was small, intimate, life-supporting, ideal for Mediterranean gregariousness. The citizens painted their houses pastel green, blue, yellow, or brown. New Orleans had learned how to waterproof with cypress shingles and clay tiles on roofs. Stucco was the new cement. Bricks provided the first rot-free foundations. The new sidewalks were paved with brick, imported cobbles, or flagstone. Crushed oyster shells, clay, and sand gave the citizens relatively stable streets. The Spanish, with less than a decade of stewardship remaining, gave the Creoles a city to remember them by, an Andalusian city, perhaps, but soon enough Creolized.

"He who would bring home the wealth of the Indies, let him first bring the wealth of the Indies with him." The ancient proverb encapsulates the Spanish experience in Louisiana of 35 years' rule under nine governors. Spain left behind more than it could ever take away. It cost King Charles $500,000 a year, on the average, to support his colony.

When the Spanish arrived in New Orleans, the city had no defense, the Cathedral was falling down, food was in short supply, and money was scarce. As Jo Ann Corrigan writes: "Louisiana enjoyed greater growth and prosperity during the last 10 or 15 years of Spanish rule than in all of its previous history." Under the Spanish the orphaned province, chronically short of food and labor, developed a productive agricultural system at long last. It shifted emphasis from two unprofitable staples, indigo and an inferior tobacco, to cotton and sugar cane.

For all its reputation for cruelty, the nation of the conquistadores showed surprising tolerance for its French stepchildren. Three governors married French women: Gálvez, Carondelet, and Miro. And New Orleans remained steadfastly French. French food, French language, French religion, French *joie de vivre* and *laissez faire* all triumphed.

The final victory, however, would be American. More than anything, the Spanish withdrew out of apprehension of the infant United States, just beginning to flex its muscles. In the last year of Spanish occupation, 265 ocean vessels left the port of New Orleans. Of these, 104 were Spanish or French, while 158 flew the flag of the United States.

Kaintocks and Keelboats: "I was raised on alligators and weaned on panther's milk! Ya-hoo!" they cried. These were the new Americans, noisy, uninhibited, uncouth, bellicose, and dirty, always shouting, picking fights, afraid of nobody, carrying on with rotgut whiskey, pistols, and women. The dignified Creoles called them Kaintocks, and considered them a menace.

After the Revolution, they began descending the river on their keelboats and flatboats, bringing down merchandise for delivery at New Orleans. Never was such a motley merchant fleet assembled—canoes, rafts, ferryboats, crude paddlewheels, lumbering scows. All were man-powered in 1785, except those pulled by mules laboring along the river banks. The Frenchmen were introduced to an entirely new vocabulary: mackinaws (skiffs), arks, broadhorns, and Kentucky flats and scows (propelled by horses and cattle on treadmills). Some piled into sandbars or went spinning off into rapids. Others struck snags (or sawyers) and plunged bottomward, holes stove in their sides.

After Yorktown, an immense migration across the Alleghenies began. There were a scant 12,000 settlers west of the mountains in 1782. By the turn of the century, there were 380,000 in the new territories of Kentucky, Tennes-

Spanish silver coins were scarce, and were sometimes cut into bits. Thus Spain bequeathed America the expression "two bits," or one quarter.

The main danger to river navigation was "snags," dead trees toppled into the river by caved-in banks. Some, called "planters," were fixed in the stream bed. Others, called "sawyers," were looser and oscillated unseen just beneath the surface.

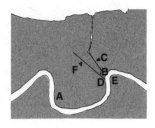

A. Boré Plantation
B. Jackson Sq. (Plaza de Armas)
C. Carondelet Canal
D. Keelboat Landing
E. Algiers Pt.
F. Canal St.

Keelboating was an eye-opening adventure to farm boys like young Abe Lincoln, who signed on for $8 a month to take a three-month trip to "Orlins" and back. It was the first big city Abe saw and the first slaves he'd seen, too. Lincoln never wrote about the trip, but he carried a lifelong memento: A scar over his right eye from a fight with thieves who bushwhacked him one night.

see, Mississippi, and Ohio. The only outlet for their produce was the port of New Orleans by way of the Ohio and Mississippi Rivers.

Kaintocks were courageous and tough. They hacked their way across mountains with Daniel Boone and Simon Kenton. Practical men, they settled on two functional vessels, the keelboat and the flatboat. The flatboat was the first river craft. It was a simple oblong ark with a shed roof, 80 to 100 feet long, able to support up to 100 tons of weight. Two great oars, or broadhorns, on each side steered it, propelling huge pens full of horses, cattle, hogs, and every kind of livestock. A typical keelboat was 50 to 70 feet long, 18 feet wide, and pointed at the bow and stern. The captain steered by a long oar amidships, while crewmen poled vigorously on each side. The keel was a massive oaken rudder, four-by-four. It wasn't elegant, but it did the job. And it could be hauled back upstream by lines to the shore.

It took three to five months of agonizing labor, fighting robbers, river pirates, Indians, and storm-driven currents to return upstream from New Orleans to Louisville. Unsurprisingly, these "children of the snapping turtle" raised unshirted hell while they were in town. Each boat had its champ or "bully," who wore a red feather as a proud sign of his belligerence. Whenever 80 or 100 keelboats tied up at Tchoupitoulas Street, bedlam ensued. One boat's bully challenged another until entire crews wound up fighting. There were two kinds of fights. A fair fight was slugging, elbowing, gouging, and kicking. The rough-and-tumble was unrestricted mayhem. It got so bloody that Kentucky passed a law in 1811 which made everything beyond "slashing" illegal.

The Keelboat Age lasted 45 years. It established the city's wide-open character—or lack of it—which attracted future generations of gamblers, fortune-hunters, con men, and grifters. It deepened the antagonism between Creole and American, and forced the final reluctant Americanization of the strategic Spanish colonial port.

The Spanish feared this American incursion and repeatedly closed the port to the Kaintocks. The *intendante* aggravated them with excessive duties and restrictions. At times, whole cargoes were confiscated. But New Orleans was too vital to be left under foreign domination.

The Dominguens: *"It was the best of times, it was the worst of times..."* In Paris, the government had fallen, the king was dead. Cries of *liberté* were heard in New Orleans theaters and cafes, yet the mood was ambivalent. Governor Carondelet moved to quell what he feared was a plot to overthrow the Spanish monarchy. Six citizens were arrested and shipped to

A Short History of New Orleans

Havana's Moro Castle prison. Fearful both of insurrection and invasion by the Americans, the governor fortified his city for the first time. A large moat and a masonry wall were constructed around the original Vieux Carré, and five forts were erected with cannons pointed in and out to meet both uprising and attack. Carondelet organized a body of 20,000 Indians to assist in his defense against the Americans, but they never showed up. Instead, revolutionary fever attacked France's most critical New World colony, sugar-rich Saint-Domingue.

Saint-Domingue was discovered in 1492 by Columbus at the western end of Hispaniola, the island on which present-day Haiti and the Dominican Republic are situated. About the size of Maryland, two-thirds of the little colony was mountain and forest land, a natural hideaway for thousands of *marrons* (runaway slaves). They hid in the treacherous hills and developed Vodun from its source in West African practice. Vodun was a complete religious system; the Voodoo which evolved in New Orleans was less complex and generally amounted to little more than black magic.

White French "islanders" from Saint-Domingue, refugees from the successful slave uprising led by Toussaint l'Ouverture, were destined to enrich the city's culture. The uprising which sent them to New Orleans was inspired by the French Revolution and resulted in Haiti's independence in 1804. The refugees were civilized, somewhat decadent people who had been lords of an island manor for more than a century. New Orleans was captivated by their easy charm, brittle wit, keen intelligence, and insight into most of the seven deadly sins. They opened the city's first theater, *Cap Français,* at Royal and Bourbon. The French-speaking Creoles were thus reinforced in their Gallic lifestyle and arrogance.

Voudun, with its elements of black magic and blood sacrifice, had inspired the slaves of Saint-Domingue. Since 1522, 12 years after the first slave arrived, there had been repeated uprisings on the island. By the end of the 18th century, the white masters were engulfed by the accumulated fury of 280 years of slavery. Outnumbered ten to one, there were perhaps 50,000 white masters, who controlled all offices, property, and privilege. Fifty thousand mulattoes served as artisans and vassals with limited privileges. The ratio of masters to slaves was ominously low. Thousands of runaways roamed the forested hills. The revolution began with a cult ceremony on August 14, 1791. There was wild dancing, a black pig was sacrificed, and all drank of its blood. Soon a half million black slaves revolted. Two hundred sugar plantations were desolated and burned. Two thousand whites were slaughtered within two weeks.

The bloody revolt on Saint-Domingue triggered the unthinkable in Louisiana. Slaves on the plantation of Julien Poydras in Pointe Coupée Parish were incited to overthrow their master, slay every white available, and lead an army of blacks downriver to New Orleans, looting and killing. The conspiracy supposedly was hatched by several white men. Someone betrayed his comrades and the plotters, including three whites, were arrested. Twenty-five blacks were killed when a band of slaves attempted to rescue them. There was a brief "show trial" and a punishment designed to demonstrate the horrible fate awaiting any slave who dared break his shackles. Twenty-three convicted men were put aboard an open boat, chained, and floated 150 miles downriver to New Orleans. At each landing, at least one was hanged. Their heads decorated poles from Pointe Coupée to New Orleans.

Following the slave revolt on Saint-Domingue, white Dominguens and free men of color poured into New Orleans seeking sanctuary. The free men of color reinforced, in numbers and talents, an already unique twilight society in New Orleans known as the *gens de couleur libre,* which soon became a sensuous and exotic part of the Belle Epoque in this most French of all American cities. Their artisans would help build the new metropolis, their sculptors would decorate it with monuments and tombstones, their fine craftsmen would become experts in hand-wrought "iron lace." Their women would become the most unusual concubines in American history, the quadroons.

Inspired by the French Revolution, Jacobins filtered into the city to urge the citizens to revolt and establish an independent republic. But much of New Orleans' energy was being taken up by progress. The first newspaper, *Le Moniteur de la Louisiane,* was published in French. It was subsidized by the Spanish government and sold only 80 subscriptions to skeptical Creoles. The city's first 80 streetlights were installed, suspended on ropes between street-corner poles. The first police department emerged, its members in cocked hats, frock coats, and blue breeches, carrying muskets. At long last, an equipped fire brigade, armed with axes, was assembled. To combat anxiety over insurrection, invasion, and the stealthy "activity of vagabonds," Carondelet organized the *serenos* or night watchmen. A Civil Guard was formed to combat "robbery and murder."

The busy governor authorized the digging of the first in a vast network of canals which one day would exceed, in number and length, those of Venice. The system connected Bayou St. John with downtown New Orleans. Carondelet boasted it was done "almost without cost." Slave labor was donated by citizens.

But the city's new prosperity was tempered by fear. Most ships jamming the harbor flew the Stars and Stripes. Slowly, the Franco-Hispanic colony was becoming dependent on American flour, coffee, soap, textiles, shoes,

Quadroon women, famed for their elegant dress, tended to upstage the Creole white women. In 1786 Governor Miro forbade them to wear plumes or jewelry. Thenceforward they bound their hair in a kerchief, or *tignon.* It became their distinctive badge of identification during Spanish rule.

and liquor.

The French drank wine as we drink water today. But the Americans then drank almost anything except water because it was so unhealthy. In New Orleans, a bottle of *vin ordinaire* was on every table. In 1793, a New Orleans druggist experimented with something different, and changed the drinking habits of North America. A. A. Peychaud dispensed a new "tonic" to clients of his apothecary shop at 727 Toulouse Street. It was composed of cognac and the product of a secret formula, eventually named "bitters." Peychaud mixed the concoction in a double-ended egg cup the French called a *coquetier*. The Americans couldn't pronounce *coquetier*, so they called it a "cocktail."

The Big Grass: Sugar plantations enriched Louisiana's feudal economy and made New Orleans the wealthiest city in the antebellum South.

An even more stunning discovery was made in the 1790s. Upriver, on Bienville's old plantation (where Audubon Park is now located), Etienne Boré, an *émigré* from Illinois country, contemplated the destruction by pest of his principal crop. With his indigo wiped out, Boré determined to grow sugar cane. Two local planters, Solis and Mendez, had been the first to cultivate the Big Grass in Louisiana, where the growing season was shorter than in the tropics. They made a syrup from the juice and an inferior rum called taffia, but they failed to granulate sugar. Boré's wife, whose father had labored unsuccessfully to granulate sugar, attempted to dissuade Etienne. His friends beseeched him not to waste his time; the climate was too cool in Louisiana.

But Boré had already planted. A sugar mill was being built and two-thirds of his total expense had been incurred. In 1795, his persistence was rewarded. Etienne Boré ground his first cane and, after a moment's silence, cried: "It granulates!"

The granulation of cane into sugar was an event comparable to the invention of the cotton gin. In southern Louisiana, sugar, not cotton, was the dominant cash crop for most planters during the Belle Epoque. Balanced on the glistening ebony backs of 60,000 slave laborers, the sugar industry would become the absolute essential to the feudal economy of the state and city. Slavery might be "the execrable sum of all villainies" to John Wesley, but to the incredibly rich landlords of antebellum Louisiana it was the engine of their wealth.

The American Era

4

Fifty French soldiers formed the guard of honor to receive the tricolor as it slowly descended the flagstaff in the old Place d'Armes. The sergeant in command carefully gathered it in, neatly folded it, and then led his men marching past the American troops. At the cry, "Present arms," American rifles snapped to attention. The Creoles watched impassively.

It was December 20, 1803. Slightly less than eight months before, the infant United States, that bluff new world citizen, had doubled its size with a few strokes of a pen in Paris. Bonaparte's new empire in Louisiana came and went in exactly 20 days.

The tricolor was carried to the Sala Capitular on the second floor of the Cabildo and was presented to Pierre Clement Laussat, Colonial Prefect for the French government. The new American governor, William C. C. Claiborne, and General James Wilkinson, military commander of the new territory, passed along the final act of cession, written in English and French. There was silence as Laussat absolved the Creoles of all loyalties to France. Still speaking French, he urged them to become American citizens. Claiborne spoke briefly in English, guaranteeing "freedom of liberty, property, and religion." The Creole Catholics listened, uncomprehending.

A roll of drums and the Stars and Stripes began its uncertain ascent, snagging at mid-hoist before finally unfurling at the top of the pole. The Place d'Armes reverberated to the explosion of rifle salutes to the United States of America. "Occupied again," the Creoles muttered. The Louisiana Purchase was consummated.

For just 20 days it had been Bonaparte's colony, the first foothold of a new French colonial empire in North America. But it was only an isolated outpost, restive and vulnerable to the Americans and British, and without a

Opposite page
Yet another flag: When the Stars and Stripes were raised in what is now Jackson Square, many new Americans celebrated. And many Frenchmen wept.

secure supply line anchored in the Caribbean. Realizing this, the Little Corporal determined to recapture Saint-Domingue from the "Gilded African," Toussaint l'Ouverture, and his legion of former slaves.

Other than Quebec and, possibly, Montreal, there was no city in North America more French than New Orleans, and the revolutionary fervor of the 1790s had inflamed many Creole citizens. The night word reached town that Louis XVI had been beheaded, hundreds rioted in the streets. Spain found it increasingly difficult to govern a French city that soon openly applauded Napoleon.

As early as 1779, the Creoles had begun petitioning France to return them to civilized Gallic society. Such agitation served Bonaparte's purpose. Spain was virtually his puppet. The once warm revolutionary bonhomie France shared with the United States vanished; an undeclared shipping war broke out between the two nations. That ardent Francophile, Thomas Jefferson, now considered the French, whose culture he so openly admired, enemies of the United States.

Quietly, Bonaparte opened negotiations with Spain, bullying the Spaniards into retrocession of Louisiana. The Treaty of San Ildefonso was so secret that the citizens of New Orleans did not find out they had been ceded for three years. (They then enjoyed 20 days of repatriation before becoming Americans.) Capitalizing on a brief, fragile peace with Great Britain, Napoleon then went after Saint-Domingue, which would be his Caribbean naval base and supply depot for New Orleans. "New Orleans," he told his advisers, "offers an empire of unlimited possibilities . . . and an effective barrier against further American settlement."

Bonaparte sent his brother-in-law, Charles Le Clerc, with 30,000 troops to "pacify" Toussaint's island stronghold. Emerging from the bloody slave rebellion of 1791 as a charismatic "Black Napoleon," L'Ouverture had declared himself "Emperor for Life." Le Clerc used treachery to lure the black leader aboard a French vessel. He was slapped into irons and spirited away to France where he rotted in a Paris prison. The move, calculated to demoralize Toussaint's Haitian guerillas, only strengthened their resolve. Ferocious jungle fighting, reinforced by a vicious yellow fever epidemic, decimated Le Clerc's army. Finally, when he could count only 4,000 French soldiers still fit to serve, Le Clerc withdrew from Haiti. Napoleon's dream of a French empire in America was, for all practical purposes, over.

Bonaparte's obvious designs on the Mississippi Valley heightened Thomas Jefferson's interest in New Orleans. The American president had written that "no such position for the accumulation and perpetuity of wealth and power ever existed." The Kaintocks, as usual, were "angry as grizzlies" over being denied use of the New Orleans port whenever the Spanish puppet governors decided to close it. "The day France takes possession of New Orleans," Jefferson wrote his minister to France, Robert Livingston, "we must marry the British fleet and nation." But neither France nor Britain could be tolerated at the mouth of the continent's greatest river. "There is on this globe a single spot, the possessor of which is the natural and habitual enemy of the United States. It is New Orleans... through which the produce of three-eighths of our territory must pass to market."

Four cents an acre: Napoleon sells Jefferson one-third of a country for $15 million.

A Noble Bargain: Jefferson instructed Livingston to put in a bid for the Isle of Orleans. He convinced a skeptical Congress to appropriate $2 million. For three years, Livingston attempted, with no success, to negotiate. Only Napoleon could make this decision, and Napoleon ducked the negotiators.

When the Spaniards suspended the precious "right of deposit," drying up American commerce on the Mississippi, the Kaintocks exploded. They offered President Jefferson two frightening alternatives: either the Kaintocks would march down the river and seize New Orleans, or the Kaintocks would secede from the United States and then seize New Orleans.

James Madison fanned the flames, sending word to Bonaparte that "Americans are men of action . . . roused to a war fever." "Seize!" cried James Ross of Pennsylvania on the floor of Congress. "Paper contracts or treaties have proved too feeble. . . . Plant yourselves on the river!" Jefferson sent James Monroe to Paris to dicker for Orleans and the Floridas, raising the ante to $9 million.

The poker playing ended abruptly in April 1803. "They [the British] shall not have it!" Napoleon told his negotiator, Barbé Marbois. He had concluded that he would rather deprive the British of more than just the Isle of Orleans. So Napoleon offered the entire territory, one-third of a subcontinent, for $15 million.

The U.S. doubled its territory with the Louisiana Purchase, but the $15 million price was about as much as the government's total revenue in 1803.

It was the best real estate deal in history. All or part of 13 future American states were carved out of its 825,000 square miles at a cost of about 4¢ an acre. But not every American was thrilled. Geographer Hugh Murray wrote of the great "Arkansas desert" stretching east from the Rockies which was "entirely unsusceptible to civilization." In Congress, Representative Griffin of Virginia proclaimed: "I fear this so-called Eden of the New World will prove a cemetery for the bodies of our citizens."

Congress ratified the Purchase, but not until the Federalists reprimanded Jefferson. They said the Constitution did not authorize land purchases by a president. It did authorize him to negotiate treaties, however, and Jefferson contended the Purchase was, in effect, a treaty, a guarantee against attack by the French and British. Jefferson later admitted that he had "stretched the Constitution until it cracked."

When the treaty negotiations concluded in Paris, Livingston turned to the French minister Talleyrand and asked: "Can't you be more specific on the boundaries?" Talleyrand's reply was prophetic: "I don't know the boundaries, but . . . you have made a noble bargain for yourselves and I suppose you will make the most of it." Napoleon commented: "I have just given to England a maritime rival that will sooner or later humble her pride."

On the evening of historic December 20, Prefect Pierre Laussat gave a state dinner and ball. It was attended by Spaniards, Frenchmen, Americans, including, in Laussat's words, "American women whose charms we have not yet celebrated." Laussat looked back on his "reign of twenty days" and said he was not dissatisfied. The Americans were left with "a vast country explored and made known to the world by France." The destiny of three nations had been irrevocably changed in three weeks' time; Laussat called it a "double revolution."

But the arrival of American forces was a time of mourning for the Creoles. Governor Claiborne spoke no French and surrounded himself with English-speaking Americans. English was proclaimed the colony's official language. So the conflict between the Creoles and the Americans began immediately. It soon spread to the marketplace and eventually to the dueling ground. But the first real confrontation occurred on a ballroom floor.

The incident took place at an ordinary public ball a few weeks after the lowering of the tricolor. Two quadrilles were formed at the same time, one French and the other English. Objecting to the French quadrille, an American threatened a musician with his cane, and there was a great uproar. Claiborne did not interfere at first, but Daniel Clark, a wealthy, Irish-born local merchant, urged him to exercise his authority.

Governor Claiborne, unable to speak French, was embarrassed. He tried to persuade the American, an army surgeon, to desist. The French quadrille began again. The American doctor interrupted again, insisting on the English quadrilles. Someone shouted: "If the women have a single drop of French blood in their veins, they will not dance!" Every Frenchwoman left the room.

Two weeks later, on January 22, 1804, Creoles and Americans squared off again on the ballroom floor. One side cried: "French quadrille!" The other replied: "English quadrille!" General Wilkinson mounted a bench and attempted, in fractured French, to calm the dancers. Claiborne pointed his finger accusingly at a Mr. Le Balch, a Creole, whereupon Wilkinson, appar-

In 1976 Cecilia M. Pizzo's suit to nullify the Louisiana Purchase on the grounds that her family's properties were illegally seized was denied. The statute of limitations, she was told, had run out 167 years before.

ently under the impression that the governor was directing him, tried to arrest the man. A fistfight broke out but ended abruptly when General Wilkinson began to sing "Hail Columbia." American cheers were drowned out by Creole voices singing the "Marseillaise," followed by cries of "Vive la France!"

Fights over the choice of French or English dances erupted in ballrooms throughout New Orleans. Claiborne's first official report to Secretary of State James Madison astonished American officials. He apologized for bringing up a matter that must seem trivial to Madison, but dancing was the "foremost concern" of New Orleanians. (Travelers from all over Europe and America were dumbfounded at the passion for dancing they observed in the Crescent City. There were 80 different dancing locations in the city by the time of the Civil War.)

One anonymous writer pretended to complain about the city's love of dancing, saying ladies often had "every other part of their bodies exposed, if not to sight, to touch."

None Dared Refuse: The Battles of the Ballroom led inevitably to the Dueling Oaks. Until the Civil War there was scarcely a man in public life who had not fought at least one duel. Governor Claiborne fought Daniel Clark after Clark became a United States Congressman. The governor's secretary and brother-in-law, Micajah Lewis, was killed in a duel by a man protesting Claiborne's policies.

Dueling in New Orleans was probably more widespread and difficult to control than in any other place in the United States. Bienville had outlawed it in 1722. Both the Spanish and French governments enacted tough laws but never enforced them. An *affaire d'honneur* could result from any slight, real or imagined. A journalist of the time wrote: "The least breach of etiquette, the least suspicion cast of unfair dealings, an aspersion against the moon, the night, the temperature . . . almost anything can provoke a challenge."

Dueling was banned in Washington in 1839. Pistols by then were so accurate it was feared Congress might have difficulty establishing a quorum.

As Claiborne and his secretary found out, "none dared refuse." The rules were ironclad, contained in an extraordinary document called the *Code Duello*. Kaintocks might settle arguments with their fists. Creoles never would. Fistfighting was considered barbaric.

The *Code Duello* carefully defined the difference between a slight, an insult, and an offense ("attacking the honor of one's mother, sweetheart, or wife"). It outlined specific methods of redress. It is interesting that the Americans called it dueling, and once thrust into it, pursued it to the death. The Creoles termed it an "affair of honor" and sought merely "satisfaction," often achieved at the first blood.

In time, Exchange Alley, connecting Canal Street with the St. Louis Hotel, was lined by a dozen *salles d'armes*, academies for sword, rapier, and

The Dueling Oaks: On the grounds of the Allard plantation (now City Park), gentlemen sought "satisfaction" with swords, rapiers, and pistols for almost 80 years.

pistol training. The great *maîtres d'armes* were folk heroes. They became legends and, in some cases, marked men.

With so many young men trained in the use of weapons, at times things got out of hand. The historian Gayarré tells of six Creole youngsters who headed home a little tipsy following a ball. Blood aflame from too much dancing and tippling, they spied a long, level patch of ground lit by a full moon. Pairing off for "some sport," tempers were quickly roused. Only four returned home.

One duelist, the greatest swordsman in Louisiana, bought his own cemetery. Don José "Pépé" Llulla, called "Master of Masters," was never successfully challenged. He put up posters in three languages, challenging anyone in the city to cross swords with him. There were no takers. Llulla purchased the Louisa Street Cemetery (now St. Vincent de Paul) when he retired, having fought 41 duels with no defeats. In his dotage, Don Pépé is said to have strolled his properties, shooting flowerpots out of the hands of his caretakers. His favorite trick, though, was breaking an egg, held by his son, at 50 paces.

One famous swordsman, Bastile Croquère, a mulatto, was educated in Paris and considered the handsomest man in New Orleans. He taught the cream of Creole society, but did not fight one duel because of his race.

A Short History of New Orleans

One Sunday in 1839, ten duels were fought under the Dueling Oaks at Allard Plantation, now City Park. Literally thousands were contested there. Another favorite spot was in St. Anthony's Garden behind the St. Louis Cathedral. Deuling became so bloody and nonsensical that professional "hit men" cold-bloodedly picked their "marks" and then blew them away with everything from shotguns to long rifles. One American, born in Maine, chose harpoons. His Creole adversary demurred, saying he risked no honor refusing to be "speared like a beast."

All sorts of weapons were used before the Civil War brought grim reality to weaponry and forced an end to these "affairs of honor." One freak combat in 1810 involved a Kaintock who called for eight-foot sections of three-by-three cypress timbers. The two duelists clubbed each other senseless.

In 1817, wealthy Creole legislator Bernard de Marigny challenged an American blacksmith, James Humble, a recently elected Representative who had never shot a gun or unsheathed a sword. Humble was close to seven feet tall and towered over Marigny, who was only five feet nine. His choice of weapons was unique: blacksmith hammers while standing in six feet of water in Lake Pontchartrain. Marigny realized immediately he was "over his head." Declaring he could not harm a man with such a sense of humor, he invited blacksmith Humble to dinner.

Bernard de Marigny once received a record seven challenges at one ball for refusing to let anybody dance with one Anna Mathilda Morales.

Creoles and Americans: "Almost all Louisianians are born French or are of French origin," wrote Joseph Xavier Delfau de Pontalba, a French-educated Creole of impeccable credentials. "It is with rage in their hearts that they have ceased to be French." The Creoles' insular society eventually would destroy them, but for a half-century it provided a defense against an egalitarian social system that threatened their supremacy and pride. Creole historians disregarded all criticism by native Frenchmen, especially Robin and Stoddard, who portrayed Creoles as backward, ignorant, indolent, insensitive, and excessively cruel to their slaves. Parisians tended to be smug and self-congratulatory at the expense of colonists. The fact is that some few Creoles were well-educated and cosmopolitan, but isolation in the swamp left many provincial and uninformed.

At the time of the Louisiana Purchase in 1803, barely 50,000 persons made their homes in the vast territory of Louisiana. On the tiny Isle of Orleans about 8,000 resided, half of them black. A stockade enclosed most of the town, with forts at four corners.

What is now Canal Street, America's widest main thoroughfare, was a ditch, or moat, part of a growing patchwork of open drainage that criss-

"Creoles are well-shaped and of agreeable figure. They are lively, alert and agile . . . endowed with a natural disposition for all sciences, art and exercises that amuse society." — Chevalier Guy Soniat du Fossat, a Creole.

Overleaf
Under the eagle: This painting of New Orleans soon after the Louisiana Purchase shows a quiet promenade on the river, cows grazing in what became Faubourg Marigny.

crossed the saucer-like city. The Cabildo, Cathedral, and French Market were located where they are now. An ugly wooden gallows stood where General Jackson's statue now stands, in the stark Place d'Armes. Until 1827, the public pillories faced the Cabildo. There thieves, wearing placards around their necks, endured barrages of rotten fruit and vegetables thrown by waifs and riff-raff.

The houses of the wealthy were generally built of stucco over wood, or brick roofed with slate or tile. The poorer class lived in elevated frame houses with shingled roofs. These were raised from eight to fifteen feet to guard against flooding and keep out alligators, snakes, wild dogs, and frogs. Some families had wells, but the water usually was unfit to drink. Drinking water was carted into the city from the river and sold for two cents a bucket. New Orleans youngsters spent hours filtering it through porous stone, or clearing it with lime, alum, or charcoal.

Ice cream first appeared in New Orleans in 1808 at the Exchange Coffee House, at Chartres and St. Louis (now known as Maspero's). Natural ice was floated down the Mississippi by flatboat and stored in insulated ice houses. This was four years before Dolly Madison served ice cream in the White House.

In 1804 Congress divided up the immense territory: everything north of the thirty-third parallel became the District of Louisiana; the southern part, conforming to today's state, was called the Territory of Orleans. Governor Claiborne, in his first report, noted that New Orleans possessed two banks, a customhouse, a navy yard, several wholesale and retail stores, a French theater, and a French newspaper, *Le Moniteur*. The first English paper, the *Louisiana Gazette,* began publishing in 1804, appearing twice a week. In 1810, it became a daily.

New Orleans was a mercantile center, founded on small trade and commercial enterprise. Business often was conducted by "sordid speculation"; usury, smuggling, and informing were also tolerated. The main products of the countryside around the city were rice, sugar, indigo, tobacco, and cotton. Plantation sawmills supplied the Indies with cypress, cedar, and maple boards and shingles.

Education was deplorable. There was no college or public library. Neither was there a bookstore. The Ursuline Convent School had 70 boarding students and 100 day pupils who paid when they could. Trademasters took a few apprentices. In 1803, perhaps 200 of New Orleans' 8,000 inhabitants could read or write passably well. Visitor Henry Brackenridge described it as "a place of speculation, dissipation, debauchery, and revel, but not much for books."

This libertine attitude may have contributed to the stereotype of Creole housewives as quarrelsome viragos. Already, many men had established quadroon concubines in small houses. Few Creole men attended church; Creole women attended every morning. Since there was only one church, St. Louis Cathedral, it's difficult to believe everyone could have fitted inside.

A Short History of New Orleans

Vegetables were dear; four turnips cost as much as two pounds of meat. Plantation owners ignored their gardens to concentrate on cash crops. Bear oil, the colonial shortening, and bread cost as much as meat. "Everywhere," said Robin, "one finds on the table small pieces of bread, no vegetables, and large pieces of meat."

For two years William C. C. Claiborne was virtual dictator of the new American possession. This 28-year-old straitlaced Protestant was perplexed by the Latin temperament. He wrote Jefferson that he thought the people "generally speaking, honest. But," he continued, "they are uninformed, indolent, luxurious—in a word, ill-fitted to be useful citizens of a Republic. Under the Spanish, education was discouraged and little respectability attached to science. Wealth alone gave respect and influence... hence ignorance and wealth generally pervade this part of Louisiana." Claiborne added a grace note about Louisiana's young females: "They are among the most handsome women in America."

The young Virginian learned French and set to work recodifying the laws and translating them into English. Since Laussat's adoption of the municipal system ignored the judiciary, Claiborne personally sat on the bench in special session. Creoles complained that he "sat as sole judge, not attended, as the Spanish governors were, by a legal advisor."

Louisiana's Civil Code of 1808 and the Code of Practices adopted in 1824 were quite different from those of any other state. Both were written in French, which "took precedence over English in case of conflict," and were based on Roman rather than English law. Scholars still debate the origin of the Civil Code. John Tucker says the Code Napoleon (1804) furnished "the basic framework with some Spanish elements interlaced."

Governor Claiborne adopted a conciliatory attitude toward the Creoles, but he could not make peace with the hostile environment. On October 5, 1804, he wrote the president: "Lower Louisiana is a beautiful country, and rewards abundantly the Labour of man. But the Climate is a wretched one, and destructive to human life." He had just suffered the loss of his 21-year-old wife, his daughter, his secretary, and many of his closest friends, wiped out almost overnight by the first awful epidemic of yellow fever. Smallpox followed yellow fever and Claiborne launched a massive inoculation campaign. Smallpox never theatened again, but yellow fever returned over and over for a century.

Claiborne's personal troubles with the pestilence continued. Five years later, he sadly reported to President James Madison that he had lost his second wife, also 21 years of age, to the fever. The miserable governor begged to be moved from his waterfront mansion. "The filth and various matter for putrefaction which accumulate near the water's edge have often proved offensive to me, even when in my chamber," he wrote. This condition arose from the local custom of throwing garbage, refuse and the contents of privies into the river. Everybody—refuse men, night soil workers, private citizens—slopped waste material near the top of the levee.

William C. C. Claiborne was appointed governor six times by Presidents Jefferson and Madison. Overshadowed by the outsized images of his contemporaries, Jackson, Lafitte, and Jefferson, he doggedly overcame intense personal hardship and staunch Creole resistance. In 1812 his efforts were rewarded when Louisiana was admitted to the Union as the 18th State. Claiborne defeated the Creole's champion, General Jacques Villeré, in the legislative election and became the first elected Governor of Louisiana.

William C. C. Claiborne was Governor of Louisiana for 13 years, longer than any to date. He overcame great personal tragedy to establish confidence in American government, if not a profound respect for Americans.

The Terror of the Gulf: Perhaps Claiborne's toughest battle was his confrontation with that swashbuckling rogue gallant, Jean Lafitte, the buccaneer. From his base on Barataria, shrouded by the mists of the swamp, the legendary Lafitte preyed on Spanish shipping and other vessels in the Gulf. He first appeared in New Orleans in 1806, and opened a blacksmith shop. There he forged iron grillwork by day and met by night to plot his schemes.

Some say Lafitte was a pirate. He defiantly claimed to be a privateer, operating under a "letter of marque" from Latin American countries that legalized his plundering. His small smugglers' ships and pirogues scooted back and forth to Barataria with men, messages, and merchandise. At one point, one thousand men were stationed there, part of a giant commune. Privateers kept detailed records of their operations. New Orleans agents received a cut, and each crew member a percentage. Lafitte's chief lieutenants were his brother, Pierre, and Dominique You, a former gunner for Napoleon Bonaparte.

Lafitte's sales outlets were spotted across the Gulf Coast, from Pensacola to Galveston. Local officials were cut in on the profits. Lafitte easily undersold any merchant on any item. His shrewd involvement of merchants and public officials made him difficult to prosecute. His "bargains" and charm attracted women of the wealthiest families, making him Louisiana's most glamorous man. He cannily profited from the conflict between American and Creole, using information from his efficient spy system to neutralize both.

On January 1, 1808, the constitutional prohibition against the importation of slaves went into effect. Slave-traders like Lafitte could sell able-bodied slaves for $800–$1000.

When importation of slaves was made illegal, the price on the "black market" soared. Despite the prohibition, Louisiana's slave population grew from 40,000 to 330,000 in a half-century.

At Barataria, Lafitte confronted his loose confederation of cutthroats, fugitives, and water-rats. He insisted they attack only Spanish ships, for which Lafitte carried the "marque," and slave ships, thus reducing the possibility of legal retribution. They called him "Bos," but he still slept with "one eye open." There were too many men like Gambi, a surly Italian who boasted that he had murdered 10 men with a broad-ax.

"The Terror of the Gulf" swept that body of water with his newly organized fleet of ships, flying the flag of Cartagena. Grand Terre, his island fortress, became a swampland metropolis, complete with cafes, bordellos, gambling dens, and warehouses. Lafitte built a mansion of brick and stone so lavish his planter clients went home raving of the "pirate's exquisite taste and style."

At one end of the island was an enormous barracoon, where slaves in chains awaited purchasers. Slave auctions were held once a week; as many as 400 blacks would be sold and smuggled off to New Orleans. There, Pierre Lafitte's store on Royal Street exhibited "trained Africans" worthy of high prices. By 1813, Jean Lafitte was supplying almost every New Orleans store with contraband. His fleet of barges commuted regularly to Barataria.

Governor Claiborne issued a proclamation denouncing the Baratarians as "pirates" and warning Orleanians not to deal with Lafitte. The buccaneer brazenly defied Claiborne, moved back into the city, wined and dined merchants, and publicly announced more illegal slave sales. Claiborne issued another proclamation, offering a $500 reward for the pirate's capture. Lafitte countered with posters, plastered all over the city, offering a $1,500 reward for Claiborne's capture. Claiborne brought in a grand jury indictment against Lafitte and his pirates. Pierre Lafitte was thrown into the calaboose, without bail. Jean Lafitte quickly demonstrated his influence by employing attorney Edward Livingston, brother of the man who had sworn in George Washington. The buccaneer paid him $20,000. He also hired attorney John R. Grymes, who later joined Lafitte for a party on Grand Terre and, while carousing all night, gambled away his considerable fee, believed to be $10,000. Lafitte engineered a jail break to free Pierre.

But America's second war with the British soon gave New Orleans more important worries. History records that the War of 1812 was, for the most part, an embarrassment to both sides. Privateering on one hand and plundering on the other was rampant. The infant American nation was defeated frequently, almost wrecked financially, and split internally. Several northern states threatened to secede. America did much better on the sea, though, and privateering greatly aided its naval campaigns. Armed merchantmen of a new type called the "Grand Turk" captured 31 British prizes.

No one knows Lafitte's true motives, but in 1814 the privateer-smuggler

Buccaneer-patriot: Jean Lafitte often appeared on "Wanted" posters, but his cannons, flints, and powder saved New Orleans.

A. Battle of Lake Borgne
B. To Barataria
C. Chalmette Battlefield
E. Furthest British advance
F. British Anchorage
G. Present-day New Orleans (shaded)

turned patriot. A British force sailed into Barataria and offered him $30,000 to join them. Lafitte refused the offer and then informed Claiborne. The Governor told federal officials he believed the buccaneer, regardless of his past.

The federal authorities ignored Claiborne's intercession. They were fed up with Lafitte's marauding sea dogs. Six American gunboats and several other armed vessels bombarded Grand Terre and caught Lafitte unaware. Most of the stronghold's buildings and nine armed merchant ships were destroyed. Jean and Pierre Lafitte disappeared into the swamp.

The Battle of New Orleans: Andrew Jackson was appalled by the precipitous federal action. It was clumsy and intemperate, apt to turn the buccaneers against the United States. General Jackson had been assigned to defend the southern coast and, in particular, New Orleans. He knew the value of Lafitte's "hellish banditti" in the labyrinthine swamps. On December 10, the British fleet, carrying 7,000 troops, anchored off Ship Island, near Biloxi, Mississippi. General Jackson hurriedly tried to erect defenses in New Orleans and moved to enlist Lafitte's help.

The Battle of New Orleans has been minimized because it was fought two weeks after a peace treaty had been signed in Ghent. Difficulties in communication kept the news from reaching America in time to halt Pakenham's army. Because of this, it has been called "The Battle That Missed The War." Historians point out, however, that the treaty was not ratified until February 17, 1815, one month after the battle. And had the British won, it would have been a worthless scrap of paper. General Sir Edward Pakenham, the Duke of Wellington's brother-in-law, commanded the finest, most experienced force in Europe. Many of his 10,000 men boasted they had "licked Napoleon once a week during the Peninsula Campaign."

When the Americans declared war on the British, it was 41 days before England knew about it. When the Treaty of Ghent was signed in 1814, there was no mention of the impressment of seamen, the right of search and seizure, or any of the reasons the war was fought.

Old Hickory was a testy man, an individualist who disliked formality. To defend New Orleans, he had to recruit everybody—Creole dandies, plantation patricians, blacks, whites, *cafés au lait*, slaves and freemen, Indians, and pirates. They were put to work digging ramparts, barricading bayous, and building a line across Chalmette, between the river and the swamp, buttressed with cotton bales.

The determined Jackson cut off the water approaches to New Orleans as best he could. But the British army and navy, incredibly, navigated shallow lakes, alligator-infested swamps, and winding, uncharted bayous for 80 miles, from Ship Island on the Mississippi Gulf Coast through Lake Borgne, up Bayou Bienvenu to Chalmette. On the night of December 23, they sneaked

A Short History of New Orleans

up on Jackson's flank and captured the Villeré plantation. Major Gabriel Villeré barely escaped, diving out a window.

Villeré brought the news to the startled Jackson. "By the Eternal," Old Hickory roared, "they shall not sleep on our soil." Caught off guard, he boldly seized the initiative and ordered a night attack on the enemy camp. His Kentuckians and Tennesseeans darkened their faces and, using rifle butts, knives and tomahawks, fell upon the British, whooping and hollering like Indians. The British had no idea who or how many Americans were lurking in the moonless night. Jackson's strategy paid off. The uncertain British regrouped and waited until their full force was assembled before attacking. By that time Jackson had finished his line.

Pakenham made two probes in advance of the main attack. The first advance, on December 28, met with heavy artillery fire and was halted. By this time, Jackson and Jean Lafitte had reached agreement. The General

Rabble vs. redcoats: Andy Jackson and his hastily assembled Kentucky sharpshooters and Gulf pirates repulsed the British at Chalmette. The painting exaggerates—the redcoats never reached the ramparts.

would intercede to obtain pardons for Lafitte and his men if the buccaneer would lend the General his guides, his powder, his flints, and Dominique You.

Dominque You, the one-time cannoneer for Bonaparte, proved an excellent marksman. He helped drive the British back on December 28, dealing fear into their ranks with precision cannonading. On New Year's Day, 1815, Pakenham's cannon replied but failed to smash a hole in Jackson's line.

Early on the morning of January 8, 1815, the British attacked. Under cover of fog, they marched in solid, well-formed lines across the open plain. Artillery fire was sporadic. Suddenly, about 200 yards from Jackson's line, the fog began lifting. Four deep, the Kentuckians stood, waiting for command. Their long rifles were deadlier, more accurate at greater distances than any the British had ever met.

Jackson gave the order and 500 long rifles opened up, loading and reloading, in rotation. Within 15 minutes, the entire British front line "melted into the ground." The pride of Britain broke and ran.

Pakenham reformed his troops and personally led them in another attack only to be shot dead from his horse. Major General John Keane attempted to rally the demoralized Britons but he, too, was shot down. At the very center marched the Royal Highlanders in full regalia. They, too, were mowed down methodically by Jackson's long rifles. Their courage in the face of "hellfire" won the undying admiration of those Americans who watched them barely reach the rampart and go down, bagpipes skirling.

The British could not believe that Jackson's hasty assemblage, barely 2,000 men—Creole gentlemen in street dress, buccaneers, Indians, blacks, and unkempt backwoodsmen—would stand together. Five months before at Bladenburgh, Maryland, the British had launched a fiery barrage of Congreve rockets and the raw American troops panicked and fled. The British had marched into Washington unmolested and burned the nation's capitol.

At New Orleans it was different. In one of the most staggering defeats an army every suffered, the English lost more than 2,000 men. Jackson counted seven dead. On January 27, 1815, Britannia sailed away, never to return in battle.

One historian says flatly that the Battle of New Orleans was "the single most conclusive battle in American history." It dramatically united the nation and confirmed its revolution. It broke America's bonds with Europe and proved to be a final defeat for British colonial ambitions in the New World. The Mississippi Valley was secured and talk of secession in New England was quelled. Andrew Jackson became president because of the battle, and a republican aristocracy gave way to Jacksonian democracy.

Pakenham's army joined Wellington in time to vindicate itself against Napoleon at Waterloo. Within two years, William C. C. Claiborne was dead at the age of 42. Claiborne's nemesis, Jean Lafitte, eluded judgment and history. Some say he prepared to settle down in the city but, sensitive to constant references to his "pirate" background, he returned to privateering. Dominique You, René Beluche, "Cut Nose" Chigazola, and Gambi sailed with him for a while, but eventually went their separate ways.

Jean Lafitte's contribution has been distorted so badly that it is difficult today to properly appraise his role in the battle that may well have saved a country. No one knows for certain what happened to the "Terror of the Gulf." Some say he fought with Bolivar and died in South America. Most probably the aging corsair returned to the only thing he really knew, privateering, from a squalid base in Yucatan. He reportedly died of fever at the age of 47, a lonely and disheartened man.

Legends die hard in New Orleans. There's a house still standing at the corner of Chartres and St. Louis streets which was supposedly built as a refuge for Napoleon Bonaparte. It was constructed between 1797 and 1814 by two French-born brothers, Claude Pierre and Nicholas Girod.

Nicholas Girod was Mayor of New Orleans when news arrived that the Little Corporal had escaped from Elba. Girod promptly announced that he intended to provide Napoleon with sanctuary. Napoleon did, in fact, attempt to seek asylum in the United States, but without success. So he reformed his army and, 100 days later, was defeated by the British and sent packing again, this time to St. Helena. New Orleans buzzed with rumors that the Little Corporal was to be rescued and given a Louisiana base by French-speaking leaders in the community. According to local legend, the Napoleon House was completed with a special cupola that could serve as lookout over the river. Special apartments were designed upstairs where Napoleon could plan another empire. Mayor Girod knew just the man to run the British fleet: Napoleon's former gunner, Dominique You.

Napoleon's rescue supposedly was supported by a syndicate of wealthy sympathizers in New Orleans, St. Louis, and Charleston. They purchased the schooner *Seraphine*, one of the fastest ships in the world. Lafitte's scurvy Baratarians were signed as crew, but three days before Dominique You was to sail, word reached New Orleans that Napoleon was dead. No one really knows whether such a plot existed at all, but then again, there's that house at Chartres and St. Louis streets.

Jean Lafitte was an international hero. Following the Battle of New Orleans, Lord Byron wrote "The Corsair," ending: "He left a corsair's name to other times/Linked one virtue with a thousand crimes!" Dominique You became a revered local celebrity. Gambi was killed while pirating in the Caribbean. René Beluche became a Commodore in the Venezuelan Navy. Nat Chigazola — direct descendant of "Cut Nose" — is a leading citizen of Grand Isle.

The city's addiction to the Napoleon mystique did not diminish after his death. Faubourg Bouligny's main street was named Napoleon. Other streets were named for his great victories: Milan, Austerlitz, Berlin, Marengo, and Constantinople.

La Belle Epoque

5

Downriver toward New Orleans, the paddlewheeler chugged, making mighty breathing noises and puffing great clouds of smoke. The steamboat *New Orleans* was churning its way into American history, headed for the Crescent City at three miles an hour, under the captaincy of Nicholas I. Roosevelt, great-grand uncle of the illustrious Teddy.

At village after village along the Ohio, townspeople lined the banks, cheering on the "fire beast." With Roosevelt was his pregnant wife, Lydia, two servants, an eight-man crew, and a giant Newfoundland named Tiger. One year earlier, Nicholas and the intrepid Lydia had travelled the same river on a flatboat, surveying every current, every rapid, snag, or eddy in advance. They covered the last leg, Natchez to New Orleans, in a rowboat.

When the Roosevelts returned to Pittsburgh after that first trip, Nicholas told his sponsor, Robert Fulton: "We can lick that river." The historic vessel *New Orleans* was built in Beelen's iron foundry, beneath a high bluff overlooking the Monongahela. Fulton's design called for a 148-foot boat, probably a sidewheeler, though some early drawings depict a sternwheeler.

All along their historic journey, the Roosevelts were pestered by premonitions of disaster. The weather turned sullen and misty, "weighing on our spirits." Early darkness and mist seemed ominous. Heavy rains caused the river to rise. Lydia Roosevelt gave birth to a child.

The Roosevelts shot the treacherous Ohio falls, spinning briefly out of control. Then, on December 16, 1811, the whole world seemed to break apart. The ground shook and cracked open, as jagged fissures slashed across level farmland. It was the most intensive, and extensive, earthquake in American history, centered at New Madrid, Missouri. The river convulsed and entire islands disappeared. The Mississippi actually reversed itself and ran back-

Robert Fulton did not invent the steamboat. Robert Fitch did, in 1787. But Fulton's *Clermont*, launched in 1807, was the first to attract commercial interest.

Opposite page
Festival of commerce: This smoky lineup of steamboats illustrates the monied bustle of the city's antebellum economy.

Shocks from the New Madrid Quake were felt 500 miles away in New Orleans. Lake bottoms raised 15 feet, the Pemisco River disappeared, ground in Tennessee sank to form Reelfoot Lake, 18 miles long.

wards for miles.

Despite earthquakes, childbirth, and skepticism, the first successful river steamboat, the *New Orleans,* finally arrived at the city for which it was named on January 12, 1812. Adoring crowds lined the levee to greet the "swimming volcano." It docked, belching smoke, and a black man threw his hat into the air, shouting: "Ole Mississippi done got her Marster now!"

"Mississippi steamboating," wrote Mark Twain, "was born about 1812; at the end of thirty years it had grown to mighty proportions; and in less than thirty more it was dead! A strangely short life for so majestic a creature." Steamboating's Golden Age lasted from 1820 to 1870. The first 40 years coincided with New Orleans' most opulent period of growth, La Belle Epoque. The "floating palaces" were so ornate, with their scrolled woodwork, gingerbread carvings, and sumptuous appointments that they were called "floating wedding cakes."

The steamboat was, in reality, a water-borne hotel with lavish lounges, daily newspapers, 100-foot-long bars, barbershops, restaurants with fancy menus offering seven soups and 15 desserts. Steamboats were a gourmet's delight and a gambler's paradise. Riverboat gamblers were dazzling dressers, brilliant psychologists, gifted liars, schemers, and quick thinkers. Some steamboat captains, absolute dictators once a ship was under way, would not leave port without a gambler aboard. It was both good luck and good business.

Each passing year, steamboats were built larger, faster and more palatial. Steamboats helped open the West long before the steel ribbons of the railroads interlaced the continent. Towns located on the big rivers grew rapidly. The cotton trade boomed and so did New Orleans, doubling its population in ten years.

Steamboats filled America with lore, legend, and lyrical names—the *American, Valley Queen, Belle of Memphis, Sultana, Silver Wave, Mayflower,* and, of course, the *Natchez* and the *Robert E. Lee.* The first packet run from New Orleans to Natchez took five-and-one-half days. By 1870, the *Robert E. Lee* made the trip in 10 hours, 36 minutes and 47 seconds.

Before the steamboat, it could take many months, rowing, poling, and warping, to travel from St. Louis to New Orleans. The first steamboats made it in 11 days.

The burgeoning prosperity of New Orleans was best evidenced along the bustling levee and wharves. In the 1830s, steamboats arrived and departed every hour. Fifty of them lined the docks at any one time and a great pall of smoke hovered over the river. A steady procession of crude arks and flatboats floated down the Mississippi, and the brigs, clippers, sloops, and schooners from faraway Havana, Vera Cruz, and Tampico, created a forest of masts along the wharves, row on row.

The levee stretched out three miles at the river's crescent, paralleled by an unbroken line of storehouses, cotton presses, and shops. Merchandise of every description—hams and horses and mules and furs and booze—was transferred by slave-gangs, singing exuberantly. "They may be miserable," commented one English observer, "but they are certainly the merriest miserables in the world."

Richard Bache, Ben Franklin's son-in-law, recalled "Negresses and quadroons carrying on their bandanaed heads, and with solemn pace, a whole Table— or platform large as a Table—crowned with goodies, such as cakes and apples and oranges, figs, bananas, pineapples, coconuts, etc." It was a festival of commerce.

Fifty thousand cotton bales could be seen almost any day, stretched out in endless rows, waiting for shipment. Cotton and sugar represented the principal wealth of the delta, where vast plantations commanded the river from Natchez to the swamp. This stretch of alluvial country was one of the richest, most productive, bottomlands in the entire world.

All America was changing, moving faster, building bigger. Frontier outposts, like Pittsburgh, Cincinnati, St. Louis, were suddenly cities. It was push, shove, and haul it downriver. Steamboats blew up almost every week. Flatboats hit snags or evil currents and went under; crews disappeared. An estimated one of every three boats destined for New Orleans never arrived.

New Orleans was the third largest city in America by 1840. Its population had soared to 102,000. It led the nation in exports, surpassing New York. The tonnage on its wharves was soon double that of its Hudson rival, and, by 1860, 3,500 steamboats were docking in New Orleans, an average of 10 a day. Two million bales of cotton crossed its wharves annually. It was called the Queen City of the South.

Creole supremacy was threatened as the city grew beyond its French Quarter stronghold. The main artery, Royal Street, retained its character— the Old World ambiance of hotels, banks, exchanges, and cafes, interspersed with elegant residences. Bourbon Street changed radically from a street of pitiful shanties to an elite avenue of fine homes. The resplendent shops on Chartres Street began moving to lower Canal Street. The Yankee invasion quickened. Faubourg St. Mary became the commercial center of the city. American exporters and importers, sugar and cotton brokers, built their own city on the other side of Canal.

Antebellum New Orleans was a land speculator's dream. Faubourg St. Mary was subdivided from the original tract of land owned by Bienville and,

The toughest place on the Mississippi was Balize Island, near the river's mouth. The first stop for raunchy, land-starved sailors, it made Natchez-under-the-Hill and the Swamp in New Orleans seem tame.

Second city: Indians still roamed the streets of "suburban" Faubourg Marigny in 1821. For a time, Marigny's house overlooked acres of empty lots and streets named Desire and Love.

later, the Jesuits. Barthelemy Lafon devised an ingenious plan for the area above St. Mary, now called the Lower Garden District. He named his streets after the nine Greek Muses: Thalia, Melpomene, Terpsichore, Polymnia, Euterpe, Clio, Erato, Calliope, and Urania. Tivoli (now Lee) Circle was meant to be an outdoor pleasure garden, an island surrounded by a circular canal. In 1833, a cluster of riverside hamlets above Faubourg St. Mary was incorporated into the city of Lafayette. Eventually, it would embrace the Garden District, one of the most delightful and historic residential areas in America.

Downstream from the Vieux Carré, the quixotic Creole millionaire, Bernard de Marigny, subdivided his plantation and set out to build his own city, Faubourg Marigny. Marigny spent more money, offended more people, and fought more duels than anyone in town. A millionaire at the age of 15, he was sent abroad by his guardian to obtain an education and cultivate manners.

A Short History of New Orleans

Marigny introduced galloping dominoes all over New Orleans. The Americans dubbed his game "crapaud" (toad) after the French—"toad-frog" being the name popularly applied to Frenchmen. Crapaud was shortened to "craps." Marigny, it's said, in a downhill battle to pay off his galloping debts, taught everyone in New Orleans how to play.

An expert with the blade, Marigny also had a rapier tongue and wit. His street names for Faubourg Marigny were classics of drollery. One street he named Craps, after the game he invented. He went on to pepper the landscape with fanciful monnikers, many of them *double entendres:* Frenchmen, Desire, Good Children, Bagatelle, Peace, History, Poets, and Music. He named the main avenue Champs-Elysées, or Elysian Fields, in homage to his education in Paris. With Jovian delight, Marigny created nearly 100 original streets from his piece of the swamp.

The streetcar named Desire ran between Canal Street and Desire Street, which originally was Desirée. The streetcar is now a bus, and today only one streetcar line —the St. Charles, oldest line in America—runs in New Orleans.

Most of Bernard's fanciful street names have disappeared. By 1850, there were three churches located on Craps Street. The congregation at Craps Methodist didn't like the way it sounded. So Craps became an extension of Burgundy Street. Eventually, the City Council changed 75 of Marigny's "classic titles."

Rue d'Amour (Love Street) led directly into Rampart Street where quadroon mistresses were "kept" by Creole gallants. They inhabited neat row cottages, after signing arrangements with Mama. Good Children Street supposedly domiciled the illegitimate offspring of Marigny's and other Creole liaisons. Greatmen Street was a sardonic inside joke on a garrulous tenant who bored him with fictitious stories of his intimate association with Napoleon, Lafayette, Jefferson, and other "greatmen."

Marigny's network of streets was soon lined with simple cottages of native-born artisans and workers, including many free persons of color. *Gens de couleur libre* were often taught a craft and sometimes educated in Paris. A battalion of free men of color fought with distinction in the Battle of New Orleans. Many became sculptors for the city's ornate Cities of the Dead, craftsmen in wrought iron, and builders. Many constructed the sturdy Creole cottages that lined New Orleans streets by the hundreds.

Two separate cities were developing above and below Canal Street. The French Quarter and Faubourg Marigny lie below Canal. The Germans arrived in the 1840s, in such numbers that Faubourg Marigny was nicknamed Little Saxony. By the eve of the Civil War almost one-sixth of the city's population was German. The Anglo community nested above Canal, in Faubourg St. Mary, the Lower Garden District, the township of Lafayette, and the Irish Channel. By 1860, 25,000 Irish were concentrated in deplorable slums along the river. The area was known as the Irish Channel because, it's said, every

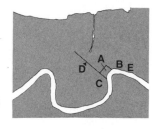

A. French Quarter
B. Faubourg Marigny
C. Faubourg St. Mary
   (business district)
D. Canal Street
E. Little Saxony

time it rained heavily, water poured down from the higher (and richer) Garden District and flooded them. Slaughterhouse and soap factories were located there, and their smell was nauseating.

Canal Street, with its wide median strip, became a dividing line. Many Creoles refused to cross it. Some daring people, from both sides, met in the middle. This middle ground was soon called "the Neutral Ground," the term used to this day for any median strip dividing a New Orleans avenue or boulevard. Canal Street was built to accommodate a 50-foot canal that was never dug.

The Americans determined to make themselves independent of the Creoles. In 1832, they built their own canal. It was a bold, back-breaking effort by 10,000 Irishmen willing to risk death by fever rather than endure famine and persecution back home. The route covered a little over six miles of *flottant* from Lake Pontchartrain to the river, forming the New Basin Canal. Their resources were few. They had no dynamite or dredges, but plenty of picks, shovels, and wheelbarrows. The infernal swamp often backed up to fill in what they dug out.

It took six years and one million dollars to finish the New Basin Canal. When it was completed, 8,000 laborers had perished. A hundred years later the City of New Orleans voted to fill it back up.

This was the golden age. Some, with a feel for its Gallic legacy, called it "La Belle Epoque." By whatever name, the antebellum awakening in New Orleans between 1825 and the Civil War was as opulent, unrestrained, and flamboyant a time as any city in America ever experienced, but the era was not unmixed with tragedy, inhumanity, even horror.

Mud and Opera Houses: Despite terrible epidemics, and the internecine struggle between Creole and Anglo, New Orleans doubled its population, and then redoubled it in less than three decades.

Aggressive and ambitious Anglo Saxons kept arriving in great numbers. Wealth was their obsession. Some dreamed of making a quick fortune, then returning to more temperate climes. Many fell in love with local ladies, or the city, or both, and stayed. It was common knowledge that if an intelligent, hard-working young man applied himself, he could start at the bottom in "Orlins" and be a business partner within 10 years.

The Anglo influence rapidly changed the city's houses from "the uncouth Spanish style to more elegant forms." Old Fort St. Charles, located at the foot of Esplanade (now occupied by the old U. S. Mint Building) was demolished. Two new markets were built, and drainage improved.

New Orleans tackled its long-time enemy, the swamp, with paving stones imported from Europe and the North. By 1835, the city had invested nearly $5 million in streets, drains, and banquettes. But when this orgy of civic pride ended, fully 75 per cent of the city was still unpaved. "After a rain," a Captain Hamilton wrote in 1833, "the centre of the street is at least a foot thick in mud." Many Orleanians grew up learning to swim in the city's gutters.

It remained for the turbulent Englishman James Caldwell, actor-builder-organizer-planner-entrepreneur, literally to "light up the town." Caldwell introduced gas lanterns, suspended on ropes or chains above the middle of the city's main streets. "At night," a visitor from Virginia noted, "a row of these burning lamps may be seen a mile long." James Caldwell might also be called the author of the central business district. Camp Street was a ramshackle shanty town when Caldwell built his first American Theatre near Poydras. For years, uptown ladies in fine silks and satins tiptoed across gunwale-planks sunk in the morass to catch the opening curtain.

In 1835, Caldwell challenged the hogwallow on St. Charles Avenue with the St. Charles Theatre, an edifice so breath-taking "it surpassed all in the world but three." Then he enlisted the builders Dakin and Gallier to attempt the impossible, a building of more than four stories on the "floating land." New Orleans' first great American hotel, the majestic St. Charles, emerged from the swamp in 1837, overlooking the pigsties and butter beans of Pierre Percy's truck garden.

By 1837, the city boasted three major theaters. No city in America loved opera so much and productions were staged in French, Italian, and English. A vigorous personal and business rivalry developed between Caldwell, the thespian, and John Davis, the man who introduced big time gambling to America.

Davis, an *émigré* from Saint-Domingue, put up a complex of buildings on Orleans Street, between Bourbon and Royal. There was the Davis Hotel, the Orleans Ballroom (future home of the Quadroon Balls), and the impressive Théâtre d'Orléans. Davis, it was said, could lodge you, feed you, amuse you, and fleece you, all in one city block.

Davis was the first man to bring plush accoutrements to a gambling house, offering "free meals and drinks" as long as you played. He insisted upon full dress in the gentleman's salon. His was the prototypical gambling palace and it attracted the nation's highest rollers. He used his profits to subsidize the finest European artists and musicians. John Davis introduced grand opera and the first regular ballet troupe. The gala opening of *The Barber of Seville* at the Théâtre d'Orléans in 1823 attracted the cream of society.

All architecture in New Orleans was once considered temporary by an anxious populace resigned to the caprices of floods, storms, subsidence, and, on occasion, the poorest sort of construction.

No American city ever witnessed more varied and reckless gambling than the Crescent City. Gambling emporia were licensed at fees of $5,000 a year, the money going to support Charity Hospital and Orleans College.

The great dome: The "sublime proportions" of the first St. Charles Hotel (1837) "strike even stoical Indians with wonder and delight," said a contemporary guidebook.

Four operas were performed each week, two *grandes* and two *comiques*, while three nights were alloted to vaudeville and musical comedy, the amusements of the hoi polloi. Davis supported opera for three decades, pouring proceeds from his other enterprises into the Théâtre d'Orleans. It finally gave way to the much grander French Opera House in 1858. The French Opera continued with few interruptions until 1919 when the opera house burned. (The site at Bourbon and Toulouse today supports the Downtowner Motel.) The French Opera House was, to a great extent, the focal point of Creole social life, the scene of balls, parties, debuts, marriage receptions. Once gone, there was no replacing it, for the Creoles were in their twilight.

James Caldwell treated life as extravaganza. Nowhere was this more evident than in his world-famous St. Charles Hotel. Built to surpass in size and magnificence any hotel anywhere, it was the tallest building in New Orleans, a six-story colossus topped by a gleaming white dome which was visible up and down the river for miles.

Architect James Gallier, who later built the City Hall, earned an international reputation for his design. The St. Charles' portico was composed of massive Corinthian columns in the Greek Revival style. The bar was octagonal in shape, and accommodated an army of 1,000 dedicated drinking men. The lower floor had space for shops and public baths, and auction rooms for slaves. Under the dome, a magnificent spiral staircase led up three flights to bedrooms, situated off spacious galleries. The St. Charles was the showplace of New Orleans for 15 years. One night in 1851 a fire broke out in the kitchen, spread through the flues, and left the hotel in ashes.

It took exactly two hours to plan the second St. Charles and less than two years to build it. The new, improved hotel boasted "the five largest mirrors in Christendom," hot and cold running water, and occasional heating, produced by an asthmatic steam engine that shook the entire building. In 1894, the second St. Charles burned down. A third St. Charles rose on the same spot and lasted 60 memorable years. It did not burn down. It was demolished in 1974, and replaced by a parking lot.

The competition between French and American culture extended to every facet of the city's life. While the first St. Charles was going up, the French Quarter erected its own deluxe pile and called it the St. Louis. The rivalry was based on more than ethnic pride. New Orleans attracted more than 40,000 transients every year. Almost half were Creoles and "foreign French," businessmen from France and the West Indies. So the French built the opulent St. Louis Hotel in the Creole style, and rushed to open it before the ballroom, the baths, or even the facade were completed. It burned down within two years.

The new St. Louis Hotel boasted a domed rotunda that was "the most beautiful in the world, even in New Orleans." Beneath the awe-inspiring rotunda, slaves were auctioned daily, from noon to three. To assure that commerce proceeded uninterrupted, management pioneered the "free lunch," hustled to the auction circle lest the planters miss a "bargain." New Orleans was the only city where slaves were costumed for auction, to enhance their saleability. It was under the rotunda that Harriet Beecher Stowe envisioned the sale of Uncle Tom."

Perhaps the fatal flaw in the introverted Creole society was that the Creoles honestly believed the world was centered on them. The St. Louis Hotel and the Exchange Bank connected to it deteriorated at almost the same rate that Creole society declined. The St. Louis was an empty, desolate hulk when it was demolished in 1915.

Piped–in drinking water, available in the 1830s, was too expensive for most people, who purified river water by putting it "into a large stone jar, a small piece of alum is thrown in, after an hour you may draw off a tumbler as clear as crystal . . . the mud adheres to the sides and bottom of the jar."

Slaves were regularly smuggled into New Orleans, as many as 250,000 in 50 years. By 1860, there were 25 slave yards, jails, or camps within blocks of the St. Louis Hotel. Lest they annoy ladies, slaves were not allowed to be displayed on sidewalks.

A City Divided: The building boom of the 1830s produced many new hotels and boardinghouses, some imperfectly constructed. New Orleans had no experience with large, heavy buildings mired in soft soil. One local architect said it was providential the St. Charles Hotel burned down before it fell down; it had settled 28 inches, the external walls were cracked, and the floors "undulated."

One hotel, the Planters, collapsed the night of May 20, 1835, killing 20.

The hotel's unreinforced wooden columns had buckled. The newspaper *L'Abeille* chided the owner for his carelessness and suggested a building code might be needed. The paper never followed up, nor did the public.

In that decade, an amazing thing happened—New Orleans literally was divided into three cities with separate governments. From the time of the Louisiana Purchase in 1803, the Americans and Creoles had become progressively more alienated. Council meetings turned into pitched battles. The Americans claimed they had been frozen out of political power. The Creoles considered them pushy, crude interlopers. Samuel J. Peters effected a compromise, weighted heavily on the Anglo side.

The Americans wanted to incorporate Faubourg St. Mary into a separate city, just as the village of Lafayette had achieved autonomy in 1832 (it rejoined the city in 1852). Peters' "curious experiment in city affairs" amended the city charter to create three separate municipalities with three city councils, three treasuries, and one mayor. The mayor was a figurehead. The real power in each "city" was the Recorder.

At the very zenith of its prosperity and growth (1835–52), New Orleans was arbitrarily split three ways and governed for 17 years by this hydra-headed municipal monster. The First District belonged to the proud Creoles, encircled in their Vieux Carré. The Second District, Faubourg St. Mary, between Canal Street and Felicity, was the citadel of the Anglo Saxon merchant princes. The Third District was the Faubourg Marigny, a potpourri of French, mulattoes, and Germans. The Mayor was "exempted from magisterial duties or rights of appointments"—that is to say, exempted from power. Once a year he showed up to preside over the Common Council, composed of aldermen from all three districts.

The three warring municipalities shared little except the Canal Street Neutral Ground. The Neutral Ground symbolized the city's plight. It was, for some time, an untended mass of weeds and debris. A few itinerant hawkers set up stands to peddle fruit and coffee. George Washington Cable called it "a place of tethered horses, roaming goats, and fluttering lines of drying shirts and petticoats."

Visitors found it difficult to understand how a thriving community could cut itself to pieces and still survive. People seemed obsessed with only two things: pleasure and making money. There was no public education and little culture except the "showoff operas, balls and ballets."

Gerald Capers comments that New Orleans' flagrant individualism, and at times suicidal bravado, stem from its Caribbean instincts as much as its Gallic heritage. It possessed a "provinciality all its own." The comments of its newspapers left no doubt that it felt an intense local pride, resented any criticism, and denied all charges that life there was any more hazardous than elsewhere.

That bravado had a basis in reality, for no American metropolis ever faced greater obstacles than New Orleans. Its difficulties were aggravated by the complacency of an absentee aristocracy that escaped town six months a year and could afford cesspools and cisterns while the poor putrefied. Property owners would not pay for improvements and the middle class hardly existed. Visitors seemed to agree: New Orleans had the best food and the worst sanitation, the longest social calendar and the shortest life span, while supporting more alcoholics, prostitutes and gamblers than any other city in America.

Voodoo: Voodoo, the "Conjure Religion," was imported to New Orleans in 1791 by refugees fleeing the revolution in Haiti. Nine thousand Dominguens arrived in 1809 as their black generals fought among themselves for power. Slavery on Hispaniola dated back to 1510, with the first black uprising occurring 12 years later. An estimated 50,000 free people of color emerged from that tortured history, as did an Afro-Caribbean rite known as Voudun.

The Voudun religion had existed in Louisiana since the first Africans arrived. It was dispersed to the scattered plantations where slaves had little chance to socialize. It was organized for the first time in New Orleans between 1790 and 1840, and became a force the ruling white class had to reckon with for a century.

Over the long history of slavery, dating back to the 1400s, thousands of cultish snake worshippers were brought to the West Indies. They carried with them the magic word, Vodu — corrupted to Vaudau, Voudoux, Voudun, Voudou, and Voodoo, sometimes, Hoodoo. That magical word embraced a complex which included the god-snake, the cult, the rites and practices, and each priest and priestess. Even the people were Voodoos.

Voodoo, with its strain of the deadly and unknowable, scared the outnumbered white settlers so much that Governor Gálvez prohibited importation of blacks from Martinique in 1778, saying they "would make the lives of our citizens unsafe." Ten years later, slaves from Saint-Domingue were banned. Three years after that, the bloody slave rebellion began on that island, accompanied by Voodoo blood sacrifices and psychological terror.

Slave life involved constant misery and pain. The "brute Negroes" worked in chains, guarded by armed overseers who whipped them freely until they were "broken." At night, the bone-weary Africans were locked in

The first legal record of Voodoo is the Gris-Gris (gree-gree) Case of 1773. Three blacks were charged with "conspiracy to poison a brutal overseer, with a *gris-gris* made up of alligator innards and herbs. The case was dropped but the ringleader, Carlos, was never released.

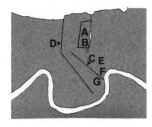

A. Allard Plantation (City Park)
B. Dueling Oaks
C. Canal St.
D. New Basin Canal
E. Congo Sq.

heavily guarded quarters. Life was less oppressive in the city, but the penalties for the mildest disobedience were equally severe.

The Code Noir provided that blacks could be branded with the *fleur de lis,* flogged, or put to death for meeting illegally. There was little relief for slaves except that which they improvised through music, dance, religious rites, and veiled laughter. When the Americans came to Louisiana they decided that the more "docile" third generation needed carefully restricted amusement. Sunday was made a day of rest for slaves, a time for amusement, religious services, and dancing. Robert Tallant says that this, "not the Civil War, was the beginning of the end of Slavery" in New Orleans.

Soon, *Le Grand Zombi* appeared. At a place called The Wishing Spot on Bayou St. John, police reported bonfires and writhing Voodoo worshippers, drunk on taffia, worshipping Zombi the snake, tearing apart chickens, shaking, quivering, leaping, and screaming until they collapsed.

Newspapers revelled in Voodoo stories, reporting any tidbit of gossip or rumor. On St. John's Eve, 1806, a white man supposedly found "his daughter in a thin nightgown, dancing with 100 half-naked blacks . . . in a room crawling with serpents and frogs . . . she wanted to get her lover back."

In 1817, the City Council passed an ordinance forbidding slaves to gather for dancing or any other purpose except on Sundays—and only at places designated by the Mayor. The Mayor selected Congo Square. For 20 years, slaves danced, sang, and performed sanitized Voodoo rites for crowds of curious locals and visitors.

Congo Square was situated where the ramparts of the city once stood, off Beauregard Square in the area now occupied by Armstrong Park. It was a large green plain lined with sycamore and surrounded by a picket fence with four iron gates. White people stood outside and gaped as slaves performed the calinda, the bamboula, and variations of African tribal dances. It seemed terribly sensual to onlookers, but the more grotesque and erotic aspects of Voodoo were omitted. The dancers did not wear traditional loincloths and bells; they sported cast-off finery obtained from their white masters.

The rudimentary first rhythms of jazz were heard in Congo Square. The Congo drums always led, accompanied by the small bamboula, and the marimba brett which combined reed and string principles. Some rattled gourds filled with pebbles and grains of corn, while others twanged Jew's harps and rang triangles. On full dress occasions, the first four-string banjos made their appearance.

The true African dance, George Washington Cable reported, "was a dance not so much of legs and feet as of the upper half of the body, a sensual, devilish thing tolerated only by Latin-American masters, given the dark inspiration of African drums and the banjo's thrump and strum." White folks, seeing these splendid productions, were relieved. They shrugged off rumors of evil gris-gris and Voodoo orgies. It was all just "darky foolishness."

Enter the Doctor: No one recognized John Montaigne for what he was. His followers said he was "descended from the night," a great Senegalese prince and sorcerer, the ordained spirit of *Le Grand Zombi*, King Voodoo—Doctor John.

A towering, coal-black Senegalese, Doctor John arrived one day in New Orleans claiming to be an African potentate. His face was fierce, with deep-set piercing eyes and masses of scar tissue at the jowls.

Doctor John *was* Voodoo for three decades in New Orleans, a sly practitioner of the occult arts, a master psychologist who also specialized in spying, bribery, extortion, coercion, collusion, and generalized mischief. He told a fantastic tale about his previous life. His father, he said, was a great African king who had scarred Montaigne's face according to royal tradition. Then the Spaniards came and sold him into slavery. In Cuba, he talked his master into freeing him. Then, said John, he travelled round the world twice and landed in New Orleans, rolling cotton on the docks.

Somewhere, the Senegalese Svengali discovered the Power. He mixed minor potions, practiced his wicked stare, saved some money and moved up to Bayou Road, alongside the rich white folks. His home contained a bizarre collection of snakes, lizards, scorpions, and human skulls. Dr. John further scandalized his neighbors by purchasing ten slaves, all female. He married some of them, performing his own "black" wedding ceremonies. In later life, Doctor John boasted that he had 15 wives and at least 50 children. He paraded the downtown streets in the uniform of a Spanish grandee. When he finally became a serious Voodoo, he wore only black, with a frilly white shirt, a cape, and a beard "forked like the devil himself."

All knowledge was Doctor John's province; he was the Power and his illiterate, semi-destitute clients believed. He left the orgiastic Voodoo dance rituals to the women. Dr. John concentrated on faith-healing, branching out into patent medicine. He specialized in hexes (gris-gris) and telling fortunes. He would place a curse, or lift one, for a fee. Heavily veiled white ladies bought love potions. Young men purchased packets of talcum to win their inamorata. Sick people bought health. Old people bought youth. Others bought anything, simply because Dr. John knew secrets, terrible secrets, that could ruin them if revealed.

The Doctor developed a spy-system so simple, so sinister, and so effec-

Voodoo dance: The cult's hypnotic rituals "conjured spells," inspired jazz, and promoted nameless fears.

Gris-gris bags, worn for protection or good luck, might contain bits of bone, colored pebbles, ground pepper. Gamblers favored a red flannel gris-gris containing a lodestone. "Goofer dust," dirt taken from a graveyard at midnight, dispelled evil spirits.

tive that it became the ultimate travesty on the romanticized relationships between White Massahs and their loving Mammies and Uncles. He paid scores of blacks to spy on their masters. Using his agents' information, he blackmailed a good portion of society, black and white, high and low. It is said that Doctor John knew more about the private affairs of New Orleans white society than anyone living in the 1840s.

The tattooed Senegalese, also known as Bayou John and John the Conqueror, was illiterate. He distrusted banks. He stashed most of his fortune, burying a reported $150,000 in his backyard. Trying to achieve respectability, he invested in two grocery stores, and failed both times. As his power waned, people cheated him out of thousands, and his harem of "wives" defected, along with many children.

Determined to be educated, Doctor John hired a tutor. It was a costly move. Showing off for a "friend," John Montaigne signed the proverbial "blank check" and awakened to find that everything he owned of real value had been signed away. Old Bayou John finally attempted a comeback at Voodoo. But he was too distrusted and too old to bamboozle anyone anymore.

Doctor John was 82, his hair snow-white, when he died. Lafcadio Hearn wrote in *Harper's Weekly:* "New Orleans lost . . . the most extraordinary character within her limits." Voodoo, however, survived and prospered under his student, Marie Laveau, the Voodoo Queen. She mixed Voodoo with Catholicism. And that is definitely another story. (See Chapter 7.)

The Quadroons: Free people of color were a distinct caste in New Orleans society from the beginning. Many were the offspring of wealthy Creoles and their concubines, educated, cultured, and proud. They stood aloof from the black slaves, who resented their "high-flown ways." Doctor John railed against mulattoes: they were "like mules, neither black nor white."

Gens de couleur libre were not really free, however. They were never given political freedom, not even the right of free speech. Some, though, were men of wealth, Paris-educated, sculptors, poets, artists. A few owned plantations and slaves. In 1846, Norbert Rillieux, a free man of color, invented the multiple effect process that revolutionized the sugar industry.

Quadroon women were often beautiful, carefully trained, and educated to become mistresses of Creole gentlemen, who vied for their attentions and sometimes fought duels over them. At the insistence of white Creole ladies, who resented their "brazen intrusions," the authorities periodically set limits on their dress and mobility.

Like most "shadow" societies, the free people of color maintained rigid class differences. There were Negroes, griffes, mulattos, octoroons, and quadroons, differences hardly remembered any more.

By 1840, there were 18,000 free people of color in New Orleans. The quadroon balls had become a fixture of Creole society. These women were anything but prostitutes. They were trained by mothers who guarded their chastity and refinement to make a "proper match" with a Creole "protector."

The quadroon balls began around the turn of the century, flourished in the old Orleans ballroom until about 1850, and died with the Civil War. They were, like the slave pageants in Congo Square, "exotic" tourist attractions. The Duke of Saxe-Weimar went home raving about the quadroons' beauty and charm. One Englishman called them the most beautiful women ever seen — "resembling the higher orders of women among the high class Hindoos, full dark, liquid eyes, lips of coral, sylph-like figures, and ease of manner that might furnish models for Venus and Hebe."

More duels were fought over ladies at the quadroon balls than anything else in New Orleans. There were murders, too, committed by quadroon males. In one year six were reported. In 1881, an order of black nuns, the Sisters of the Holy Family, purchased the Quadroon Ballroom. The Sisters placed this inscription above the old ballroom stairway: "I have chosen rather to be an object in the House of the Lord than to dwell in the temple with the sinners."

Just as they legitimized slavery in the Code Noir, and dueling in the Code Duello, the Creoles institutionalized *plaçage*, affording their quadroon *placées* certain rights. When a young Creole fancied a "free woman," he first satisfied her mother he could support her. Then he established a little cottage on St. Ann Street or Rampart, in the quadroon section of the Vieux Carré. The arrangement usually ended when the young man married. A financial settlement was made and the lady married another quadroon or went into the boardinghouse business.

The children of these liaisons were often well cared for and better educated than many whites. But Creole paternalism's darker side was pernicious: quadroon men were excluded from quadroon balls and were frequently scorned by quadroon women, who themselves were ostracized by Creole ladies. Grace King wrote that "in regard to family purity, domestic peace, and household dignity" the quadroon women were "the most insidious and deadliest foes the community ever possessed."

A white woman was empowered to have a quadroon flogged on almost any pretext. Submerged rage ran deep beneath the prim, corseted exteriors of Creole women. Their upbringing was so restrictive that the first time a Creole woman shared the same room alone with a man was on their wedding night. Marriages were strictly by arrangement, made in drawing rooms, not in heaven.

As constricted as life could be for free people of both colors, it was never

"History has buried these people," Anne Rice writes of the free people of color in her novel *Feast of All Souls*. "The close of Reconstruction was the death knell for their class and with a rising tide of racism . . . the spirit and genius of the *gens de couleur libre* was forgotten."

anything but dismal for slaves. A few plantation owners suffered sufficient pangs of conscience to "will" their slaves freedom. The master of Destrehan Manor, Thomas Henderson, attempted this, but the system foiled him. A judge declared Henderson's will ambiguous and awarded his slaves to his blood heirs. Most emancipations were conveniently posthumous, leaving others to worry about any problems.

John McDonogh: John McDonogh was an intriguing exception. He was not an abolitionist; he bought and he used slaves. By the standards of the South, however, he was a dangerous radical. He treated his slaves humanely, educated them, trained them in a craft, then freed them. As a result, the Baltimore-born Scot was treated like a pariah, scorned and ridiculed as a "miser" so cheap he rowed across the Mississippi daily rather than pay the ferry fee.

There is no record that McDonogh, who owned a large plantation across the river from New Orleans in Algiers, ever sold a slave. There *is* a remarkable series of records showing that he helped slaves, financially and in other ways, to leave Louisiana as free men and women. It was planned emancipation; McDonogh usually kept them 14 years and then freed them.

As early as 1842, 19 years before the Civil War, 80 of McDonogh's liberated slaves left port bound for Africa. Others stayed and built houses for local citizens. Some ran his sugar plantations. McDonogh had the unusual idea that blacks worked better under black supervisors, and stubbornly refused to employ white supervisors or field bosses.

McDonogh violated every rule whites considered vital to guard against insurrection. "They [slaves] were my men of business," he wrote. "They enjoyed my confidence, collected my rents, leased my houses, took care of my property and effects of every kind. Those I retained were men of honesty and integrity, and I trained them in a trade for a new life." McDonogh's critics pointed out that every slave he directed to do white man's work saved him a pretty penny.

A staunch supporter of the new Republic of Liberia, he shipped trained ex-slaves back to Africa, more or less steadily, until his death. McDonogh boasted that they left with "money, clothes, household implements, and agricultural tools of every kind." It was not unusual for 80 per cent of the passengers on a ship bound for Liberia to be John McDonogh's "educated free men."

In his youth McDonogh had been quite a *bon vivant*, living in a swank townhouse at Toulouse and Chartres. He was a volunteer in Beale's Rifles during the Battle of New Orleans. Some say he was twice rejected in love and became a recluse in the wilderness across the river. Others say he was obsessed with the idea of founding free schools for the poor and, at the age of 37, decided there was limited time left to make his fortune.

John McDonogh made his fortune. He also became the most ridiculed man in town. Cartoonists pictured him as a combination of Midas and Scrooge, a skinny, gold-hoarding introvert in a tattered coat. Children were told to stay away from him. Yet McDonogh was preparing to will his fortune to the children of New Orleans.

The public school system of New Orleans exists today as the legacy of John McDonogh. When he died in 1850, he was worth over $3 million—the equivalent of about $100 million today. With 610,000 acres, he was the richest man and the largest landholder in Louisiana. He left the cities of New Orleans and Baltimore, his birthplace, about $1.5 million. (Schools could then be built for $30,000 or less.) Free schools for the poor were his bequest, and in the next 90 years, the McDonogh Fund financed the building of 35 schools bearing his name.

His tombstone in McDonoghville cemetery is carved with his maxims: "Time is Gold, throw not a minute away." "Never Spend but to Produce." "Remember always, labor is one of the conditions of our existence." Another condition in his will was more controversial. McDonogh freed all 300 of his slaves.

The "miser" who avoided people and scared children, and fraternized with his black workers also called for "free, compulsory education, guaranteed by the government and a system of general taxation to support it. . . . New Orleans is destined to become one of the greatest cities in extent and population the world has ever seen." This was John McDonogh's legacy.

In truth, New Orleans prospered so well during La Belle Epoque, that it became the wealthiest city, after New York, in the United States. It was also probably America's unhealthiest city, about to experience the convulsive phantom horror local citizens called the miasma, or Bronze John.

In 1898, a monument to John McDonogh was placed in Lafayette Square. The inscription read: "To John McDonogh from the Public School Children of New Orleans." It was paid for by school children's nickels and dimes and pennies, collected between 1892 and 1896. Since then, McDonogh Day has been celebrated by millions of students each year.

The Desolate City

"Multitudes began the day in apparently good health, and were corpses before sunset." So wrote the Reverend Theodore Clapp, for 35 years a heroic Presbyterian minister in New Orleans. His memoirs afford us the finest personal witness to the "inconceivable horrors" of yellow fever and cholera.

On the morning of May 28, 1853, the bilingual *Bee/L'Abeille* carried the headline: "Disease an Obsolete Idea." The editorialist wrote confidently: "The future is Glorious. Imagination can scarcely conceive a more brilliant destiny for the City of New Orleans!" Certainly, the winter of 1852–53 had been a prosperous one. The once squalid port town was now a bustling metropolis of 150,000 people. There had not been an epidemic of yellow fever in six years in a city once called "the pest hole of the world."

That night, the first man died, jaundiced at the eyes. Doctors couldn't believe it; yellow fever was rarely observed before August. In early June, several more cases bore the familiar markings—the wretched vomiting of blood, the yellow eyes, the black tongue. City officials dismissed them as "miasmic," products of the unhealthy fogs, "damps," and vapors.

Swamp "miasma" was the all-purpose word used to describe the combination of noxious elements, natural and man-made that, for six months each year, imperiled the Isle of Orleans. New Orleans' death rate, swollen by periodic epidemics of malaria, cholera, typhoid, and Yellow Jack, was twice that of most large urban areas.

The city was filthy. Its mostly unpaved streets were below sea level and flooded readily during heavy rain. The only sewers were open drains, clogged with garbage, refuse, and human waste (euphemistically termed "night soil"). Citizens would not drink the river water, preferring to use their backyard cisterns, breeding grounds for the *Aedes aegypti* mosquito, carrier of

"The mortality from yellow fever in New Orleans exceeds that from any epidemic that has raged in a civilized community," states James Parton in a study of epidemiology.

Opposite page
City of the dead: In 1853 half the population lay stricken, dying, or dead; the rest mourned the 11,000 victims of Yellow Jack, but formal funerals were banned.

the deadly fever.

Despite 12 devastating epidemics in 35 years, the city government had been paralyzed by its three-way division of 1836. Mayor A. D. Crossman continually was rebuffed by the Council on health measures. Merchants opposed any suggestion that an epidemic might occur. No New Orleans doctor wanted to be the first to make such an announcement and "create a panic that destroys the city commerce." On July 2, Dr. Abner Hester took his chances. "There have been," he publicly announced, "25 deaths from yellow fever this past week." The *Orleanian* angrily denied such hysterical talk.

Two hundred and four more victims of Bronze John died the next week. The hapless Municipal Council sought a quick scapegoat and impeached James Jollis, the city street commissioner. The death toll climbed relentlessly. By mid-July, 429 people had been buried and the *Crescent* finally conceded that the unusually rainy, cool weather might portend a "sickly season." The death toll was more than 10 a day when Mayor Crossman demanded that the Council set up a Health Commission. The Council obliged by voting $10,000; then, unbelievably, it adjourned itself for the rest of the summer.

The city's bells were ominously silent. Following the 1822 epidemic, an ordinance forbade the tolling of church bells and the chanting of priests during funerals. The bells "produced a depressing effect on the sick and a terrorizing effect on the well."

Doctors groped blindly for a solution, without the faintest understanding of the cause of the disease. They vainly tried bleeding, vomiting, sweating, and blistering. The so-called "heroic school" forced large quantities of mercury into the system, sometimes killing the patient before the fever could. One doctor deluged the sufferer with bucket after bucket of cold water.

The Howard Society was named for the 18th-century English reformer, John Howard. Its 170 New Orleans members were clerks and other middle class citizens who aided the sick.

"The whole city was a hospital," wrote William Robinson, a member of the Howard Society. "Confusion and delay at the cemeteries were unavoidable. The sun's heat and putrid exhalations were sickening to the senses. Tar was set on fire around and in the cemeteries, and lime profusely thrown on the cracked and baked earth covering the coffins in the trenches."

The streets were jammed with makeshift hearses, drivers yelling: "Bring out your dead." Shallow graves were dug by torchlight and quickly filled in; if it rained decayed bodies floated up.

"This city is within the Walls of Death," Mayor Crossman announced, in apocalyptic tones on August 8. Over 200 people had died the previous week. All night long, the creaking wheels of the death-wagons rattled across the cobblestones. Each evening artillery fire shook the city. "The combustion of tar and gunpowder" was supposed to clarify the atmosphere and disperse the miasma. Some nights, the tarpots blazed so intensely, the downtown streets "shone bright as daylight." Theodore Clapp reckoned that such useless ritual may well have "scared some to death.... It was," he said, "an awful spectacle to see night ushered in." Great clouds of smoke hung suspended over the beleaguered city like a funeral pall, disputing darkness itself.

Fifty-thousand of the more fortunate, one-third of the total population, left town that summer. They headed for the Gulf Coast of Mississippi or the health spas and pine forests at the other side of Lake Pontchartrain. The poor stayed behind. Almost half of them were infected. More than 40,000 cases of yellow fever were recorded; doubtless many others were not. Of the 100,000 persons who could not leave the city, at least 10,000 died. For years, it was said that in summertime there were only two classes of Orleanians: The "Getaways" and the "Can't Afford to Getaways."

In August 1856, a hurricane killed more than 200 vacationers at Last Island, a few miles off the Louisiana Coast. Many were wealthy Orleanians escaping Bronze John.

Twelve to fifteen people died every hour. The Mayor, deserted by many of his "officials," tried everything. Bedding and clothes were burned, adding to the awful pall of smoke suspended above the town. Sulphuric acid was sloshed over homes visited by death, and disinfectants poured into privy vaults. Bodies and coffins floated about city cemeteries for lack of burial and corpses rotted in trenches. Crossman recruited gangs of slaves. For some reason, blacks did not seem to succumb as often to Bronze John. Neither did Creoles, who claimed childhood immunity and who suggested that drinking wine, instead of water, helped fortify them against infection.

On August 20, 1853, 269 people died of yellow fever. It was called "The Black Day." One hospital was abandoned. Most of the patients were dead; the rest had fled. All businesses, banks, and stores were closed. The streets were deserted by all but those engaged in the business of death.

In his remarkable memoirs, based on experience in 12 epidemics, the Reverend Clapp says that the disease appeared to peak at that point. "Perhaps there is no acute disease less painful than yellow fever," he wrote, "although there is none more shocking and repulsive to the beholder. Often I have met and shook hands with some blooming, handsome young man today, and in a few hours afterwards, I have been called to see him with profuse hemorrhages from the mouth, nose, ears, eyes and even the toes; the eyes prominent, glistening, yellow and staring..." Clapp praised the Sisters of Charity, the Roman Catholic priests, and the young men of the Howard Association. "Their devotion to the afflicted bordered on the fanatical" and not one came down with the fever.

Yellow fever was a great unsolved mystery of the 19th century. Every third year, on the average, it struck New Orleans with epidemic ferocity. In the six years following the 1853 epidemic, 12,000 more Orleanians died.

Medicine remained ignorant of its secret carrier, the *Aedes aegypti* mosquito. After the 1853 plague, one physician announced that the deadly agent was a "wingless animalcula" that floated around each summer. Two other doctors said that "terrene poison" escaping from the swamp was the agent.

Cities of the Dead: Mark Twain once said: "New Orleans has no real architecture except that which is found in its cemeteries." The city once was called "The Wet Grave." The ground was so soggy that shovels struck water 18 inches below the surface. Graves filled with water as quickly as they were dug. Orleanians determined to build tombs so strong, so resistant, nothing in nature would move them. They adopted the Spanish custom of above-ground burial.

New Orleans' water table was less than two feet below the surface, and graves were watery. John Pintard wrote in 1801: "A body is speedily devoured and transmigrated into crayfish or catfish... who in their turn supply some future banquet."

Great, gleaming white Cities of the Dead are now interspersed among living neighborhoods—row upon crooked row of whitewashed vaults and ovens, a necropolis of over 20,000 in the two oldest graveyards alone, St. Louis Number One and St. Louis Number Two. The wealthy are housed in magnificent granite and marble structures, designed by specialists known as funerary architects. The poor lie honeycombed in horizontal cells, tier upon tier, built into whitewashed brick cemetery walls.

An English visitor was horrified. "They bake their dead in ovens," he said, "like we do our brown bread." The locals called them "ovens" and used them again and again. Each has a depository at the bottom called a *caveau*, where bones are placed to make way for a new coffin.

It is said that two things, dueling and yellow fever, forced the expansion of land-poor New Orleans. Metairie Cemetery was laid out on the grounds of the old Metairie race-track where the two greatest thoroughbreds of their time, Lexington and Le Compte, ran their famous match-race in 1854 before 10,000 pedigreed sportsmen. Charles Howard, a non-pedigreed millionaire, was denied access to the posh Jockey Club and swore a peculiar vengeance. "Some day," he said, "I'll buy your damned racetrack and turn it into a cemetery!" Howard did, and his neo-Grecian tomb now rests on the club-house turn.

Lafcadio Hearn wrote in 1878: "It is rather ghastly to have death in the midst of life as we have it in New Orleans. They are hideous Golgothas, these old intra-mural cemeteries of ours. [Elsewhere]... horror is masked and hidden. Here it glares at us with empty sockets."

Nearby is the Moriarty monument. A tall, winged column supports four life-sized female statues—Faith, Hope, Charity, and Mrs. Moriarty. Josie Arlington, the notorious Queen of Storyville (the first legalized red light district in America), built a marble tomb for $17,000. Out front a statuesque bronze virgin pounds eternally on the door. Everyone knows it's a virgin because Josie would never let her in.

The old pirate, Dominique You, was buried, with full military honors, in St. Louis Number Two. Not far away, in St. Louis Number One, is the tomb

Highrise graves: Burial above ground was necessary on *le Flottant*, the floating land of New Orleans.

of the Voodoo Queen, Marie Laveau, still found marked with red brick slivers and adorned with Voodoo fetishes. The two brides of Governor William C. C. Claiborne, both dead at 21, also found their rest in St. Louis Number One.

Children grow up next door to Cities of the Dead, and cheerily decorate ancestral tombs. On All Saints' Day, families descend on familial plots, white-wash the houses of the dead, cut the grass and place "immortelles" on the graves.

A New Orleans graveyard is apt to be ornamented with cross after cross, stone or wrought iron, stone lambs and iron wreaths, small bas reliefs of flying angels, blowing trumpets, statues of weeping widows and sad-eyed children. In Metairie a statue of a weeping dog rests at the foot of his master's grave.

The Pontalbas: Five major buildings, all historical landmarks, adorn the old Place d'Armes, or Jackson Square. One family is responsible for all of them. Don Andrés Almonester y Roxas, the penniless Spanish *émigré* with royal connections, built the Cathedral, the Cabildo, and the Presbytère. His fiery daughter, Micaela Leonard Almonester, Baroness de Pontalba, built the other two, known as the Pontalbas.

The red-headed Micaela inherited her father's spunk. Her marriage to

Baroness Pontalba: Survivor of two murderous bullets, she built two of the city's most famous landmarks.

Joseph Celestin, Baron de Pontalba, was arranged when she was 15 years old. She saw her husband for the first time when he arrived from France to marry her. They shared a large fortune, three sons, and not much else.

The newlyweds moved to the family chateau outside Paris. One night her father-in-law went berserk and shot the Baroness four times in the chest. He shot twice more, missing her, and then raged into his bedroom and killed himself. Somehow, Micaela survived. When she recovered, she left France and the horrors of that night behind her.

Back in New Orleans, the Baroness determined to build two row houses on the Almonester property on each side of Jackson Square. For each building, she planned 16 shops on the ground floor and 16 apartments on each of the next two floors.

The Pontalba Buildings would re-establish Jackson Square as the city's main shopping area. Micaela hired the renowned James Gallier as her designer, but they argued constantly. Gallier walked out, unpaid, leaving drawings and specifications the Baroness did not hesitate to use. The Baroness haggled so effectively with the notable architect Henry Howard that he drew up her plans for only $120.

The Pontalbas have no special reference to any period. They are a reflection of the Baroness' personalized contracting, grand design, and parsimony. This strong-minded woman drove her work crew to finish both buildings in less than two-and-one-half years.

She autographed them with a monogram, AP—for Almonester-Pontalba—set into the cast iron gallery railings. They were finished on schedule: the Upper Pontalba (St. Peter Street) in 1850 and the Lower Pontalba (St. Ann Street) in 1851. The Baroness brought them in for about $300,000. (In 1930, the WPA spent $900,000 renovating them and, in 1982, the City plans to spend $10 million.)

Baroness Micaela Pontalba next launched a drive to change the name of the Place d'Armes to Jackson Square. A handsome equestrian statue was cast by Clark Mills, mainly with money contributed by the Baroness.

Slavery: The late 1850s were alive with promise and peril. Slaves, 330,000 of them, fueled the hungry engines of Louisiana's antebellum agriculture. New Orleans was the depot for the South's human traffic. Under the rotunda of the posh St. Louis Hotel, slave auctions were conducted daily while lunch was served around the auction block. Importation of slaves had been illegal since 1807, but black cargoes still poured in. Some shipments were made up of free blacks kidnapped and smuggled in from the east. Newspapers featured page after page of classified ads for field hands, washers, cooks, mulattoes, griffes, quadroons. Near-white women brought the highest prices. The *Picayune* advertised: "Octoroon girl remarkable for beauty and intelligence." She brought $7,000.

Prime field hands brought $1,500. In one year over $2 million was "invested" in choice human property. The humane *Code Noir* had gone by the boards, and slave law in the 1850s resembled that of other slave states. The new law was simple: The slave was bought or sold like property, any time his master wished. He could not own property himself except as his master allowed. Slave could not legally marry. They could not testify in court. They could not defend themselves against a white assailant. It was a crime to teach a slave to read or write.

The entire economy of the South was built upon slave labor. In Louisiana cotton and sugar were the chief sources of wealth. James Marston Finch makes this comment: "By one of the great ironies of history, the American democracy took control of this imperial colony [Louisiana in 1803] at the moment when the cotton gin was converting America into the greatest slave power in the world. The gin had changed cotton from being a fiber more expensive than silk into the cheapest fiber on earth; and the impact of this change, rich land, mechanical ginning, and Negro slavery, combined to produce very rapidly a powerful new ruling class, the most arrogant and insular *nouveaux riches* in American experience."

> A black man, Norbert Rillieux, saved slave-owners a fortune by inventing a process for boiling cane in vacuum pans, retaining the vapor to heat other pans.

New Orleans became the great emporium of the "Slavocracy" and the city grew, despite abysmal losses to epidemics, from 8,000 in 1803 to 168,000 in 1860. The old Creole city was reluctantly bound to the Anglo-American plantation system economically, if not culturally. The upstate planters depended upon the city's factors (agents), merchants, and bankers just as the city's businessmen depended increasingly upon the planters.

> New Orleans was the largest city in the Confederacy, and the sixth largest in the United States in 1860. Almost 40 per cent of its citizens were foreign-born. Of the city's 24,000 blacks, almost half were free.

There were, at one time, Louisianians who declared openly that slavery was an evil. But, like Thomas Jefferson, they could not imagine any other way the two races might live together. Later, after slave insurrections terrified them into silence, the humanists stopped criticizing slavery altogether or began defending it as a "positive good." The absolute dependence of the Southerner upon slavery, not only for field labor but for a thousand crafts and conveniences, eventually made slaves of those who owned them. They could not conceive, after a while, of living without their Mammies, their Uncles, their Toms and Neds, for whom they often manifested a quite genuine attachment and childish affection.

Slave owners developed an unshakeable belief that slavery was divinely sanctioned. Those who criticized it were considered atheistic fanatics. Slav-

T. Brooke F.S.A.

A Short History of New Orleans

ery, they stoutly maintained, had created a much better society than the sweatshop and ghetto of the industrial North. By 1860, there was no possibility of compromise.

Newspapers carried notices of runaways almost every day. Professional slave-catchers swarmed the swamps chasing them, armed with chains, whips, guns and packs of yelping bloodhounds. Notices such as this appeared regularly: "Found in St. John the Baptist Parish—a Negress named Rosalie, between 50 and 60 years, having an iron collar with branches. She doesn't remember her master's name." The iron collar fit tightly around the throat, an inch wide with three branches curving up toward the face. Sometimes, brass bells were attached. The collar was often worn for weeks, sometimes for life.

There were slave insurrections, but they were put down quickly and savagely, so as to leave an indelible impression. In 1853, an English school teacher, James Dyson, nearly fomented a revolt in New Orleans. Dyson ran a school for boys "of color" which was a front for the black underground. There supposedly were 2,000 members ready to participate in an uprising. Someone stumbled onto a group of women making cartridges, and Dyson and the ringleaders vanished. The newspapers offered wild speculation: "Within a few days the entire city would have been in the hands of the slaves . . . the whites probably massacred."

Vigilantes patrolled all black gatherings and encampments. "White folks fearful scared," opined one old slave. Black churches were closed. A nine o'clock curfew was established.

Thanks to slave labor, New Orleans was the largest cotton market in the world. Its banks ranked first in capital stock, deposits, and specie among those of the 15 slave-holding states. Its total trade, in 1860, amounted to an eye-bulging $324,000,000. Its wharf tonnage was double that of New York City. Transshipment point for all exports flowing downstream, it monopolized commerce from the Mississippi Valley. But beneath the prosperous surface, tides of conflict were boiling.

Secession: Nowhere in the South were Southern rights or slavery defended more vigorously than in New Orleans. At the same time, trade with the states of the northern Mississippi Valley was essential to the city's prosperity. The national election of November 6, 1860, proved crucial. Louisiana voters rejected Abraham Lincoln overwhelmingly but they still favored compromise on secession. When a state convention was called to consider the issue, it split between the "cooperationists," opposing imme-

The most fabled runaway was Squire, called Bras Coupé because of an amputated arm. He haunted the swamps until killed, and his body was displayed in Jackson Square.

Opposite page
Lunch was free: In the rotunda of the St. Louis Hotel, auctioneers sold paintings, bales and barrels of goods, plantations—and slaves, often costumed to enhance their appeal.

diate secession, and those who "could not live with Lincoln."

The pulpit eloquence of the Reverend Benjamin Palmer upset the balance. A fiery orator whose sermons regularly appeared in print, Palmer defended slavery, saying freedom would be the "Negroes' doom." Southerners had four cardinal points of duty in this moral crisis, he thundered, "to ourselves, to our slaves, to the world, and to Almighty God."

South Carolina withdrew from the Union on December 20, 1860, soon to be followed by Mississippi, Alabama, and Florida. From Washington, Senators Judah Benjamin and John Slidell telegraphed: "Secret attempts being made to garrison Southern ports . . . reason to fear surprise from Gulf squadron. The danger is not from St. Louis, but from the sea." Governor Thomas Overton Moore was so sure of Louisiana's eventual secession that he prematurely seized four federal arsenals guarding the lake and the river, declaring it his public duty "to prevent a collision between Federal troops and the people of the State."

On January 29, 1861, the Louisiana legislature voted to secede, 113 to 17. "A perfect furore of enthusiasm" swept New Orleans. Bells rang and guns fired salvos from the foot of Canal Street. The Pelican flag of Louisiana appeared all over town. For 60 days, Louisiana was a "free, sovereign, independent" state awaiting formation of the new Confederacy. "The Union is dead," trumpeted the *Picayune,* "and with it all the hopes and all the fears that divided and agitated our people."

The city revelled in its sovereignty. It was the largest and richest metropolis in the Confederacy, with close ties to England; many in New Orleans felt its position was secure. War was by no means certain, but, if it came, they believed it would quickly end in victory for the South.

The United States Custom House and Mint were seized. A six-man diplomatic corps was sent to Montgomery for the Confederation convention. A new flag, worthy of an independent republic, was designed and unfurled on February 12 to a 21-gun salute in Lafayette Square. A large crowd cheered patriotically as it fluttered in the breeze: 13 blue, white, and red stripes with a yellow star in a red field. This banner, soon to be replaced by the Stars and Bars, was the fifth flag to fly over New Orleans in 142 years.

Governor Moore selected the high command for a newly created Army of Louisiana. Braxton Bragg, who had resigned from the Army in a pique over the election of Jefferson Davis as president of the Confederacy, was reinstated as Major General. This in turn offended the proud and talented Creole, Pierre Gustave Toutant Beauregard, newly returned from serving one week as superintendent of West Point. Beauregard had been engineering officer for Louisiana defenses for 10 years and had supervised construction of its river forts. He proudly declined second in command and, in a grandstand gesture, enlisted as a private in the Orleans Guard.

Before the haughty Creole left for Charleston and a Confederate General's commission, he cautioned the military to look to the city's river defenses and to arm Forts Jackson and St. Philip with the heaviest guns possible. On March 25, Louisiana became a member of the Confederate States of America. The afternoon of April 12, the telegraph sputtered the momentous news: "Beauregard Fires on Fort Sumter."

Pierre Gustave Toutant Beauregard was a Creole aristocrat born at Contreras, a lovely plantation home in St. Bernard. Chivalric and arrogant in the Southern tradition, his name was as ceremonial as his manners. One of the most colorful of all the Confederate generals, Beauregard was involved in every important phase of the Civil War from Fort Sumter to the defense of Richmond.

Beauregard: The dashing Creole general planned New Orleans' sea defenses — but left for Bull Run and Charleston before Admiral Farragut arrived.

Beauregard ordered the first shot fired at Sumter, and then helped to rout the Union army at Bull Run, the first major battle of the war. He led Confederate troops in the first major western battle at bloody Shiloh. His long, skilled defense of Charleston against sea attack was masterful. Beauregard defended the southern approaches to Richmond in 1864, and in the waning months of a lost cause, joined General Joseph Johnston in a futile effort to halt Sherman's march to the sea. Inclined at times to petulance, he was a cavalier of the Old South, the only Creole General. Orleanians revered him and called him their Napoleon in Gray.

The Yankee rout at the first battle of Bull Run and subsequent Confederate victories convinced Orleanians the Federals could never threaten New Orleans. When Federal forces landed on Ship Island, in the Mississippi Sound, the *Crescent* defiantly asked: "Why do they not come along? . . . Chalmette's glories will be repeated . . . with such a race of sneaking imbeciles as the Bull Runners of the North."

The river was blockaded and General Mansfield Lovell took charge of the city's defense. He constructed breastworks all the way around it, blocked the bayous, and laid an underwater log boom across the Mississippi, designed to stall Federal gunboats in a crossfire between the two Confederate forts, Fort Jackson and Fort St. Philip.

Too late, Richmond commissioned a pair of 16-gun dreadnaughts, the *Mississippi* and the *Louisiana*. They were still unfinished when the Yankees attacked. The city's defenders seized 14 steamboats, and armed and protected them by cotton bales, timbers, and iron rails. This "riverboat fleet" proved more ornamental than useful. Most New Orleans troops and half the fleet abandoned the city and moved upstream to Vicksburg. Only 3,000 ninety-day

A. **Ft. St. Philip**
B. **Ft. Jackson**
C. **Camp Chalmette**
D. **Old U.S. Mint**

The union commander said the Louisiana and the Mississippi "would have sunk everything that came up" the river had they been completed in time.

militia remained in the city, poorly trained and pitifully armed. "We are virtually defenseless," Governor Moore complained.

"It was incredible," writes historian Charles Dufour, "how casual the Confederacy was about defense of its greatest city, New Orleans." On April 10, 1862, Governor Moore wired the Confederate Secretary of War: "The forts can be passed. We are disorganized, and have no general officers to command and direct." Next day, Attorney General Judah Benjamin, an Orleanian whose own plantation was in the direct line of attack, calmly assured Moore that "the fleet is not destined for your city."

The Fall of New Orleans: Federal leadership was convinced that mortar fire could reduce Forts Jackson and St. Philip. A Union fleet of 40 warships, "the most powerful ever assembled in the United States," sailed from the east coast under the command of 61-year-old David Farragut. Two hundred and forty-three guns afforded him almost twice the firepower of the two forts. General Benjamin Butler followed with 18,000 men in transports.

It took three weeks to nudge the ponderous gunships over the bar at the river's mouth. Farragut commenced bombarding Fort Jackson and Fort St. Philip the night of Friday, April 18. For 96 hours he rained over 13,000 shells on the Confederate bastions, but with little effect and only four casualties. The morale of the garrisons was damaged more than the forts. The Confederate fleet of seven vessels engaged the Union flotilla on April 24. In two hours, all but one was sunk, run ashore, or abandoned. Farragut lost only one ship and three gunboats as he swept by the Confederate forts, leaving them at the mercy of Butler's army. Only two small batteries at Chalmette stood between him and the defenseless city.

New Orleans panicked. Fifteen thousand bales of cotton were burned on the levee. Empty steamboats were impulsively put to the torch and sent downstream to greet the Union fleet. The Federal Custom House was sacked and confiscated goods were burned on Canal Street. Ten million dollars worth of property was destroyed. Warehouses were looted, and all means of transportation were seized by the military. Three thousand militia commanded by General Lovell fled 70 miles north to Camp Moore, leaving New Orleans an open city. Lovell said he wished to save the city from siege, and noted that his raw trainees were "mostly armed with indifferent shotguns."

Governor Moore and other officials left by steamboat in the night. On April 25, the Federal fleet arrived and anchored off the wharves of the South's greatest city. The river was swollen and very high; riding 18 feet above the

sunken town, the Union guns pointed ominously down on the fretful population. It was raining hard as two Union officers came ashore, braving an angry, abusive crowd. Someone in the crowd fired shots, apparently aiming at a local Unionist, but, miraculously, no one was killed. For five days, Farragut tried to work out a surrender. Mayor John T. Monroe, a former stevedore and a hero of the working class, coyly refused. Monroe insisted he could not "surrender" since New Orleans was under martial law.

That Saturday morning, a small Union landing party raised the United States flag over the Mint. The last resistance caved in Sunday when the isolated Fort Jackson garrison spiked its guns, mutinied, and took off in small boats for the swamp. Fort St. Philip also surrendered. Farragut came ashore with a regiment and wheeled two howitzers into position at Lafayette Square. Determined to establish Federal control with force if necessary, he hoisted the

The night the war was lost: The Union fleet sweeps past Forts Jackson and St. Philip, laying the city open to "Beast" Butler and the Yankee occupiers.

American flag as the sullen crowd watched. Mayor Monroe came out and stood defiantly in front of one howitzer's muzzle. "There is not one in my entire constituency so wretched a turncoat he would willingly trade places with you," Monroe taunted Farragut. The crowd cheered, but that was all.

On May 1, 1862, General Benjamin Butler strode into New Orleans history, destined to become the most hated man ever to set foot in the city. He was accompanied by 18,000 troops, an army of occupation that would rule New Orleans for the remainder of the Civil War. Counting the Reconstruction period, Federal troops would dominate the city's life for 15 years.

"New Orleans is a conquered city," Butler proclaimed, "conquered by the forces of the United States . . . and lies subject to the will of the conqueror." For seven and one half months, he ruled with an iron hand. Two newspapers quietly disappeared, two were suspended, and two others became mouthpieces for the Union.

Ben Butler gave a bookseller who displayed the mock skeleton of a Yankee soldier two years in jail. Judge John Andrew was imprisoned for allegedly "keeping a small cross made of a Union soldier's bones." A Mrs. Phillips was banished to Ship Island for laughing when a Union funeral cortege passed her house.

The man Orleanians called "Beast" Butler is best remembered for his General Order Number 28, the infamous Woman Order. He was outraged by New Orleans ladies who delighted in wearing Confederate colors on their hats and dresses, whistled or sang Southern songs while passing Yankee soldiers, and left rooms, omnibuses or church pews whenever Yankees entered. Lower class demoiselles were bolder: they sometimes cursed or spat at the occupying army.

Butler's Woman Order proclaimed that any woman who engaged in such behavior would be treated as a common prostitute, plying her trade. Upon complaint by any Yankee soldier, any local woman could be arrested, held overnight in jail, arraigned the next day, and fined five dollars. Even northern newspapers were outraged at Butler's vindictiveness. Lord Palmerston stood up in Parliament and denounced it as "infamous." Jefferson Davis declared Butler an outlaw, and put a price on his head. Some ladies—Butler called them "she-adders"—reportedly gained revenge by pasting "Beast"Butler's picture in the bottom of their chamber pots.

Butler took on the clergy with the same pugnacity. A Union officer was shot down by a sniper. Butler became enraged when his funeral procession was jeered by local crowd and the Episcopal curate failed to show up for services. The conqueror "occupied" Christ Church and replaced its rector and vestrymen with Union officers. Before he was through, 40 Protestant churches closed their doors.

Butler met his match in the Reverend James Ignatius Mullon. Father Mullon was 69 years old, born in Ireland, and pastor of St. Patrick's Church. As a teenager, he'd been a sailor during the War of 1812. Father Mullon supervised the construction of the towering 190-foot St. Patrick's Church on

Camp Street. When Butler decided the Union needed metal to sustain the war effort, he confiscated freely, including fine silverware, winning further immortality in New Orleans as "Spoons" Butler. Finally, he ordered the seizure of all church bells in the city, to be melted down for Yankee cannon, and Father Mullon drew the line. "Let Butler come get St. Patrick's bell if he dares!" Butler did not dare. Many of his troops were Irish Catholics. He was too much of a politician to risk offending them.

"Beast" Butler was a corpulent, brilliant attorney, one of Lincoln's political generals. His loathesome image as conqueror was reinforced by a "cock-eye" that did not track with the other. Reared by an ambitious widowed mother, he was egotistical, energetic, and shrewd. "In war as in peace," one historian comments, "Butler was a P. T. Barnum character. Gross in body, he was unscrupulously clever in mind . . . and incorrigibly political in purpose."

Butler demanded that every New Orleans citizen swear allegiance to the Union. He enforced a scrupulous respect for the flag and for his soldiers. His occupation was a humiliation for most residents, but it did have certain benefits. Butler boasted that he spend $50,000 a month feeding 10,000 black and white refugees from the countryside. He provided work for the unemployed by detailing them to clean up the filthy city. Butler's clean-up campaign gave New Orleans the first thorough scouring it had ever received. For three years of Yankee occupation, yellow fever virtually disappeared. The city was clean, healthy—and hostile. General Butler's brother cleaned up, too. A. J. Butler called himself a colonel even though he was not a member of the armed forces. He allegedly made $2 million in New Orleans speculating in cattle, sugar, and cotton. "Beast" Butler also was accused of profiteering but he was cleared by an army investigation.

Butler's dictatorial ways finally brought his downfall. He attempted to force his authority on the city's large alien population. He was convinced some of them were trading with the Rebels and he demanded all foreigners take the oath of allegiance to the United States. The international repercussions were tremendous. Lincoln quickly countermanded the order and reprimanded Butler for his flagrant disregard of international law. The War Department condemned Butler and deplored "corruption" in the Department of the Gulf.

On December 14, 1862, the reign of the Beast ended in New Orleans. He was replaced by Nathaniel Banks, former Governor of Masaschusetts and another "political" general. Butler sailed for New York City on Christmas Eve. His farewell address to the people of New Orleans was a classic of impertinence and self-justification:

"I do not feel I have erred in too much harshness . . . I might have

When Butler bullied Father Mullon for "refusing to bury Yankee soldiers," the priest retorted: "Me, refuse to bury a Yankee soldier? Sir, I stand ready to bury the entire Northern Army."

smoked you to death in caverns as were the Covenanters of Scotland by a royal British general, or roasted you like the people of Algiers were roasted by the French; your wives and daughters might have been given over to the ravisher as were the dames of Spain in the Peninsular War, and your property turned over to indiscriminate plunder like that of the Chinese when the English captured their capital; you might have been blown from the mouths of cannons as were the sepoys of Delhi... and kept within the rules of civilized war as practiced by the most polished and hypocritical capitals of Europe. But I have not so conducted!"

One of those New Orleans ladies he termed "she-adders" sent him her reply: "We have always regarded you as a monster in whose composition the lowest of traits was concentrated; and 'Butler the Brute' will be handed down to posterity as a byword, by which all true Southerners will remember thee, monster, thou vilest of scum."

Reconstruction: Defeat and occupation was a harrowing experience for New Orleans, more traumatic than the Civil War itself. The occupation of the city ended in chaos 15 years after its capture with "unreconstructed" New Orleans an armed camp on the brink of another civil war, equipped with two governors, two legislatures, and a desperate Federal military commander striving to save face.

The river had been blockaded during the war. Cotton rotted on the wharves. Trade came to a standstill. Most New Orleans banks failed. Louisiana, the richest state in the antebellum South, became one of the poorest. Many of its 1,400 plantations were destroyed. Sugar production virtually stopped. Slaves either followed the emancipating armies or wandered about aimlessly looking for work.

Ex-Confederates were in power briefly after Appomattox. Their Black Codes restricted civil rights and, Northern radicals said, reduced "Negroes to peonage." Some Northerners favored a "hard peace" for the South, others worried about the future of four million ex-slaves, and almost all were eager to establish the Republican Party in Dixie. New Orleans became a mecca for speculators and opportunists from the North, carpetbaggers, and their Southern counterparts, the scalawags.

Charles Sumner, the eloquent senator from Massachusetts, said Confederate states such as Louisiana had committed "state suicide." Representative Thaddeus Stevens of Pennsylvania insisted they were "conquered provinces," to be run any way Congress dictated. A coalition of radical white Republicans and newly enfranchised blacks—backed by Federal troops, the

Some Carpetbaggers were idealists, some were Republican loyalists, many were opportunists, and most became blatantly corrupt.

A Short History of New Orleans

real governing force of occupied New Orleans—seized power by controlling the ballot and disenfranchising whites. For 12 years, the city suffered what George Washington Cable called "a hideous carnival of profligacy."

Violence broke out in downtown New Orleans in July 1866. When a group of freed black men, "preceded by a brass band," marched across Canal Street to attend a rally at the Mechanic's Institute, there was a melee. Someone fired a shot. Police were said to have opened fire "wildly" into the marchers. Thirty-seven men were killed, 34 of them black. One hundred and thirty-six were wounded, 119 of them black. Former Governor Michael Hahn was wounded and two Protestant ministers were shot dead. This kind of uncontrolled violence led to the repressive Reconstruction Acts of 1867 and the return of an occupying army. Its commander was the Civil War hero, General Philip Sheridan, military overseer for the entire Fifth District.

Sheridan interpreted election laws so zealously that only half the white male citizens could vote while all black males were guaranteed the ballot. Under federal supervision almost twice as many black voters were enfranchised as white. The Black and Tan Convention of 1868 (all but two of 98 delegates were Radical Republicans) created a model constitution, calling for equal justice, equality in public schools and on common carriers. It was supremely idealistic, politically opportunistic, and patently unenforceable without the presence of Federal troops.

There followed the first civil rights demonstrations, precursors of the sit-ins and protest marches that would occur 100 years later. It began in the summer of 1867 when William Nichols, a black, attempted to ride an all-white streetcar and was ejected. Other sit-in attempts were made the next two days and that weekend, a mob of 500 blacks stoned the segregated "star cars." One protester hijacked a streetcar and defiantly drove the empty vehicle through the city to the shouts of supporters.

General Sheridan resolved the situation by calling together the mayor and officials of the transit company. The meeting did not last long. Sheridan announced that all had agreed to "desegregate" New Orleans streetcars immediately.

The Radicals never put their laws into effect in country parishes. Blacks, conditioned to the whip of plantation life, were too fearful and deferential, and Federal troops too far away. It was different in New Orleans. At least 20,000 educated "men of color" were accustomed to freedom. The majority of former household slaves enjoyed liberties unknown to rural blacks. They wanted desegregation, legally and officially. And they were prepared to battle for the ballot.

In 1868, Henry Clay Warmoth, a 26-year-old self-confessed scalawag,

Perhaps the finest local writer of the last century, George Washington Cable was one of the few who dared advocate simple justice for Blacks. This "anti-Southern" attitude and his "slurs" against the sensitive Creoles caused Cable to leave New Orleans under attack, never to return.

Black Pericles: Lieutenant Governor Oscar Dunn might have been governor had he not died mysteriously; some say he was poisoned.

was elected governor. Oscar J. Dunn, a respected, able black, was lieutenant governor. Warmoth, a charming opportunist, later defected to the white Democrats, bragging that he had prevented the "Africanization" of Louisiana by vetoing or watering down Black and Tan legislation. In fact, Warmoth did anything he pleased; the governor possessed virtually unlimited power to appoint local police, election boards, and registrars. The election boards could throw out any votes, or overturn an election result. Graft became epidemic; there was wholesale bribery, crushing taxation, general plundering, and inevitably, racial violence.

Warmoth cried out, almost gleefully: "Dammit. Corruption is demoralizing down here. But it's the fashion." The 1872 election was so confused no one could be certain who was the winner, or how many votes were cast, or counted. Two different election boards named two different winners, and for four years Louisiana had two governors, Republican carpetbagger Henry Pitt Kellogg of Vermont and white Democrat John McEnery. Kellogg had the support of President Grant and was inaugurated with the help of Federal troops.

"In every election from 1868 to 1878," historian Joe Gray Taylor states, "there was so much fraud, intimidation, and other skulduggery that it is impossible to say who won a majority of the votes actually cast—or who would have won had an honest election been held."

By 1874, Louisiana was bankrupt. Its debt was $53 million. Under punitive federal and state laws, many white citizens were forced to pay exorbitant taxes. State funds were systematically plundered by Republican carpetbaggers, who kept power by manipulating the blacks and conniving with federal occupation forces. In New Orleans, the sheriff made 37,000 property seizures in two years. Thirty thousand people left the city. The presence of Federal troops inevitably provoked insurgence. Organizations like the Ku Klux Klan, the Knights of the White Camellia, and the White League were formed.

The White League was born in New Orleans in June, 1874. Only a skeleton unit of Federal troops was still stationed in Louisiana. A paramilitary organization, the league was bluntly dedicated to purging the state of Republican carpetbagger government and returning control to white supremacists. It drilled regularly at night in secret places, grew rapidly in numbers, and armed itself to the teeth. There had already been two ugly confrontations in North Louisiana when the steamboat *Mississippi* chugged into New Orleans on September 12, 1874. It was carrying a large consignment of weapons and ammunition. Governor Kellogg's Metropolitan Police, a predominantly black unit, was ordered to block any attempt by White Leaguers to claim the arms.

Few American battles have been contested under stranger circumstances. The battlefield was the central business district and its main boulevard, Canal

Street. The battle itself was publicized in advance. Downtown stores closed before noon and crowds milled about the streets leading to Canal. Camp Street was barricaded with barrels and logs; at St. Charles, 15 street cars were overturned and used for breastworks. Cheering thousands spilled out of every downtown doorway. By 3 P.M. a Mardi Gras atmosphere prevailed as the Governor's Metropolitans formed a phalanx blocking the levee.

The White Leaguers quickly outflanked the Metropolitans by maneuvering unseen behind a moving freight train. Kellogg took refuge in the U. S. Custom House, American territory. It turned into a rout, as Metro troops, confused and leaderless, withdrew. From the first round of gatling fire, the Battle of Canal Street had lasted 15 minutes.

"War!" trumpeted the *Picayune,* "So ends the Kellogg Regime!" The victorious White Leaguers easily dispatched the Metropolitan Police and hastily assembled black militia. They seized 1,000 rifles, gatling guns, and two howitzers, and then "occupied" the State House. McEnery became Governor of Louisiana (for two days) and the next night, White Leaguers staged a gigantic victory parade.

It all ended soon enough. President Grant, fearing massive insurrection, sent in several regiments of federal troops, and parked three naval vessels off the foot of Canal. The Radical Republicans were restored to office. But the message was very clear. No Radical Republican government could stand again without the overwhelming presence of the United States Army.

After 12 years of federal occupation, the citizens of New Orleans were now ready for a fight. The White League was armed and militant. The election process had become a farce. Three years later, it ground to an absolute standstill. Again two governors claimed office: Democrat Francis T. Nicholls, a much-wounded Confederate war hero, and Stephen B. Packard, a carpet-bagger and native of Maine. The corrupt Republican election board declared Packard the winner. General Nicholls went ahead and took his oath of office before 10,000 wildly enthusiastic supporters at Lafayette Square. Packard was quietly sworn in at the St. Louis Hotel, political beachhead for the Northern "invaders."

And so, for a spell, Louisiana had two governors, two state capitols, and two separate legislatures. The White Leaguers renamed themselves the Continental Guards and swung into action again. Three thousand armed men marched on the Cabildo, the old seat of government. They seized the Supreme Court, the police station, and the city's arsenal. New Orleans was on the verge of complete anarchy. To some, it was civil war. Finally, the election of 1876 forced an unprecedented resolution.

With two separate state administrations, Louisiana sent two separate sets

Freedom on a sugar plantation: Twenty years after Emancipation photographer George Mugnier took this portrait at the Evan-Hall plantation.

Francis T. Nicholls was a Democrat; no Republican served as Louisiana's governor until David Treen was elected in 1980.

of presidential returns to the electoral college in the 1876 election. So did Florida and South Carolina. In each case, one group of electors certified Rutherford B. Hayes as the winner and the other certified Samuel J. Tilden. This situation, unique in American history, was not foreseen in the Constitution. It was resolved pragmatically behind closed doors by national party leaders in a remarkable political horse trade.

The Democrats agreed to accept the Republican Hayes as president provided Hayes agreed to withdraw all federal troops from Louisiana, Florida, and South Carolina. As part of the compromise, Francis T. Nicholls, hero of the War between the States, a one-armed, one-legged relic of the moribund Confederacy, became the Governor of Louisiana.

A Short History of New Orleans

Federal troops left New Orleans on April 24, 1877, exactly one week shy of 15 years from the time "Beast" Butler first imposed his brand of military government. Reconstructon was over.

Reconstruction in Louisiana was an abysmal failure. At best, it was a grand illusion, noble in theory, impossible in practice without the force of arms. At worst, it degenerated into a thoroughly corrupt political competition with blacks as pawns, dupes, and scapegoats. The freedmen were promised everything yet wound up with little more than a subtle form of bondage. They ended up with no vote, no education, no leaders. Two-party politics was replaced by one-party Democratic rule, tightly controlled by rural planters and big city bosses. Negrophobia became the prevailing theme of political life.

Let the Good Times Roll

7

New Orleans' studied decadence after Reconstruction fascinated visitors. At the same time, muddy, unpaved streets and pestilential open sewers invited visitations of cholera and yellow fever. In 1878, more than 27,000 Orleanians contracted Bronze John and 4,000 died. The plague swept upriver to Memphis where it killed 3,500.

Cotton, sugar, and grain continued to pass through its port, but New Orleans was far from prosperous. Badly governed, it remained unhealthy, corrupt, and buried in debt. But its citizens laughed at adversity and made a virtue, and eventually an industry, out of vice. At one point, 83 gambling houses were in operation, with police "protection." Drinking and prostitution flourished around the clock. When a Sunday closing law was enacted, the state attorney general, without blinking, judged the law illegal—in New Orleans. He didn't bother to give a reason.

Drinking was pursued with fervor, and saloons easily outnumbered churches. "Our people must have their drams," snickered the *Picayune*. "They would rather let their fish and meat spoil than miss their cooling drink." One pub owner boasted that he brought $100 worth of ice a day down the Mississippi by barge just to cool his customers' libations.

Big-time gamblers stunned reformers when they secured passage of a bill illegalizing gambling. Their intent was later clarified when they began paying double "protection" to police, thereby closing down their small-time competition.

The Carnival season had been celebrated for over a century with fancy, costumed *bals masqués* (masked balls). These were Creole inventions, and spawned much jealousy when quadroon mistresses sneaked in, disguised. In retaliation, Creole wives masked and slipped into the quadroon balls, hoping

On St. Charles Avenue, between City Hall and Canal Street, there were 40 round-the-clock gambling resorts, whimsically known as "The Forty Thieves."

Opposite page
Mardi Gras: Maskers parade on Royal Street. During Mardi Gras you can be anyone or anything you want — even a dog can dress up with a ruffled collar.

to catch their husbands in flagrante delicto.

Once the Protestant Americans recovered from their shock, they joined in, and the first street processions were seen. In 1827 a group of young bucks, home from Paris, cavorted in costume. The first formal parade in 1837 was described as "outlandish and grotesque" by the *Picayune*. It occurred the same year as the Panic.

In 1838, the first carnival float appeared, a "giant fighting cock that waved and nodded its head, while drawn through the streets by a team of horses." This time the reviews read: "A beautiful joyous cavalcade... the whole town doubled with laughter." Maskers pitched the first "throws"— little sweetmeats—to their ladies.

Carnival almost failed to last through the 1850s, with bands of thugs pelting people with sacks full of flour, three major yellow fever epidemics, and political violence. The bilingual *Bee/L'Abeille* declared: "We hope we've seen the last of Mardi Gras." In answer, Comus, the god of revelry and mirth, burst forth Mardi Gras night, 1857, in the city's first torchlight parade. Comus rode one float and Satan the other, while 80 little devils danced on the street below. A black band set the tempo, and dancing flambeau-carriers lit up the night.

The Civil War called a temporary halt to Carnival, but it began again. In 1872 one of the world's great playboys, the Grand Duke Alexis Romanoff Alexandrovitch, arrived in the United States intent on shooting buffalo. He was travelling incognito as Lieutenant Romanoff. Three ships of the Imperial Russian Navy accompanied him wherever he went, which made that somewhat difficult to do.

In New York City, the Grand Duke attended a performance of the musical comedy *Bluebeard*, starring the ravishing chanteuse, Lydia Thompson. The Grand Duke was instantly smitten (he was smitten with considerable frequency). He especially loved a silly little song Lydia sang called "If Ever I Cease to Love." One verse tickled the imperial funnybone: "If Ever I Cease to Love... May fish grow legs and cows lay eggs... If Ever I Cease to Love." The Grand Duke checked Lydia's itinerary and found she planned to play New Orleans the week of Mardi Gras. He re-routed himself accordingly.

New Orleans sensed opportunity. No one had ever staged a daytime parade. Carnival boasted three different "kings," but no supreme ruler. The Rex organization was hastily formed. Banker Lewis J. Salamon raised $10,000 and was awarded the scepter. He borrowed his costume from a traveling Shakespearean troupe. Somebody donated a horse. A reviewing stand was erected at City Hall, and royal colors were selected—purple (justice), green (faith), and gold (power). The Grand Duke Alexis, ineffectually disguised as

Carnival was almost closed down during Reconstruction when Comus satirized the Carpetbaggers and depicted Grant's cabinet as a collection of monkeys, spiders, and gargoyles.

One ball: And another, and another—Mardi Gras has always been continuous festivity.

A Short History of New Orleans

Lieutenant Romanoff, mounted the reviewing stand to cheers.

In an explosion of noise, music, and color, the first Rex parade came rollicking down the avenue. Hundreds of maskers wearing costumes from the Varieties Theatre had been recruited for the grand march. A cavalry of riding lieutenants escorted a fat, gaily decorated bull. This was the symbolic *boeuf gras* of French Carnival tradition, the last meat before the austerity of Lent began.

No one counted, but there must have been 5,000 marchers by the time Rex, monarch of merriment, greeted the Grand Duke. Some inspired souls transposed the music of Lydia's song into a band tempo. Band after band delighted the imperial roué by playing "If Ever I Cease to Love," over and over. It immediately became the theme song of Mardi Gras.

"If Ever I Cease to Love . . . May the Grand Duke Alexis . . . Ride a buffalo in Texas . . . If Ever I Cease to Love."

History records that the Grand Duke stayed on to hear Lydia Thompson sing his favorite tune in person and was further smitten. It also records that Lydia left and the Grand Duke stayed. He couldn't get enough of New Orleans—and especially of San Francisco's Lotta Crabtree, star of *The Detective.*

As expanded today to more than 60 parades and countless shindigs, Mardi Gras is a time when every laborer and bank president can become, or pretend to become, brothers under the mask.

Proteus on Canal Street: The Carnival Night parade in 1883 featured floats and flambeaux smoke and fireworks. The first big parade was in 1857.

The Voodoo Queen: Fifteen years of Yankee occupation had left New Orleans largely unreconstructed. The most dramatic evidence was the annual rites of St. John's Eve conducted along placid Bayou St. John by Marie Laveau, the Voodoo Queen. So great was her influence among blacks and whites, she became known as "The Boss Woman of New Orleans."

"There are 300 Voodoos in this city," the *Picayune* editorialized on June 25, 1873. "They are presided over by a Queen . . . and amongst them are numbered at least ten white women who partake in their hellish orgies. There are about a thousand more who secretly have faith, and practice on the sly."

Voodoo was African in origin, mixing animism, witchcraft, and Christianity. Its frenzied, often obscene rites were secret, outlawed by a fearful white populace. A brickyard on Dumaine Street was supposedly the first meeting place, before Marie's lavish rituals became major public events at what she called her "Wishing Spot" on Bayou St. John.

Marie Laveau, a free woman of color, was born in Saint-Domingue in

Voodoo was dominated by women; about 80 percent of the cultists were female.

1794. She came to New Orleans in 1809, one of 10,000 whites and *gens de couleur libre* escaping the bloody aftermath of the slave insurrections. She was 15 years old when she arrived. Ten years later, she married Jacques Paris, a refugee freedman. As far as we know, she remained faithful and bore him 15 children, including a daughter, Marie, who was almost her look-alike. The awe-inspiring Doctor John was her mentor in Voodoo.

New Orleans was divided in its opinion of this beige "sorceress"—she was both a she-witch and an angel of mercy. She nursed the wounded at the Battle of New Orleans and comforted yellow fever victims during the repeated epidemics. She visited prisoners on death row, built a chapel for them, decorated their quarters.

Each June 24, in a sort of Walpurgis Night on the Bayou, she danced with her "venomous" 20-foot snake, Zombi (which was probably no more than 10 feet long and harmless). She beheaded live roosters, reportedly drank their blood, and cavorted with half-naked bamboula dancers in an outdoor orgy that caused "thousands to shudder" at its animal intensity. On June 25, 1873, the *Picayune* reported: "She tossed a chicken, feathers and all, into a pot . . . which, when mixed with other ingredients, formed a vile potion . . . which, when drunk, supposedly kept you from the Evil Eye. Such rites in this Christian Age should not go unpunished." (Eight years later, upon her death, the same paper wrote: "All in all, Marie Laveau was a wonderful woman. She died with a firm trust in heaven.")

Marie Laveau had started as a hairdresser, operating in the finest private homes. Her customers were relaxed and charmed by her manner and they talked about everything. Soon she knew who kept mistresses on the sly, who was impotent, who was alcoholic, which families showed tendencies toward feeblemindedness, which families were concealing that sinister "touch of the tarbrush."

Superstitious citizens, white and black, staked her to a quick reputation. She charged common folk $10 a visit, which was guaranteed to get a lover, hold a lover, or get rid of one. Her clients in politics and public life were charged much more for her advice. One judge paid $1,000 for a long-range vision, plus exclusive "information." Her spy system was remarkably accurate; her payroll included the hairdressers, butlers, chauffeurs, maids, stablemen, and the cooks of her clients. Marie had something on everyone, including her spies. "She was the real Boss of New Orleans," one old black told Robert Tallant, author of *Voodoo in New Orleans*. "She was big and well-built . . . men used to go kind of crazy looking at her."

Voodoo ceremonials were her public showcase, but the big money came from intrigue. The Zombi snake-worship, black cats, blood drinking, and simulated fornication were gradually phased out. She began adding Roman Catholic touches—incense, statues, holy water. Voodoo, she insisted, was not devil worship; so she offered Voodoo to God.

The Voodoo Queen put most of her rival queens out of business. One hauled Marie into court for publicly assaulting her with an umbrella. Marie beat the rap with the help of an understanding judge, an appreciative press, and an interracial army of fascinated observers who found her Voodoo exciting and contagious. Laveau always invited the press, police, and "sporting bloods" to special "functions" and she presided imperiously over Congo Square rituals each Sunday like the Queen she was.

Her house at 1020 St. Ann Street was crowded with clients. She hoodooed and voodooed, placed curses and removed them, told fortunes, and dispensed gris-gris. Marie consorted with crocodiles, they said. Marie talked with Lucifer. Marie could get whatever she wanted. She could be two places at once—with the help of her look-alike daughter. In old age the Voodoo Queen underwent an astonishing conversion. She renounced her faithful snake Zombi, all her roosters and black cats, denied any further connection with Voodoo, and returned to her mother Church. Newspapers, attentive for 50 years to her every movement, now proclaimed her "a modern Magdalene."

Marie Laveau was almost 90 years old when she died in 1881. George Washington Cable called her "one of the great sorceresses of all time." A *Picayune* writer added a subtler touch: "Much evil dies with her but should we not add—a little poetry."

Evidence of Voodoo practices still turns up in New Orleans. From time to time in St. Louis Cemetery Number Two are found beheaded chicken carcasses, plates, glasses, beeswax candles, and coconuts (settings for a ritual feast), and occasionally a rag doll with pins stuck at strategic spots.

Redeemer Extraordinary: The Radical Republicans, villains of Reconstruction, were replaced by a new and native breed of politician in the late 19th century. Far from stamping out corruption, they streamlined and legalized governmental theft and plunder. An unholy alliance of upstate planters, New Orleans "Ring" politicians, and corrupting special interests, developed one-party electoral fraud which was more effective than anything the Carpetbaggers had ever achieved.

These Democrats smugly called themselves "Redeemers," an ironic term. They established the notorious convict-lease system well before any other Southern state, reaping vast profits from the sale of convict labor, which provided fewer safeguards for blacks than slavery at its most inhuman. These new "Bourbons" were avowedly reactionary. They preached hatred of Yankees, love for the Confederacy, and a paranoid fear of the "niggers."

In 1868, the carpetbag legislature had established a state lottery, as a way of reducing Louisiana's staggering public debt. Instead, the Lottery (see also page 129) became the chief means of financing Bourbon political campaigns. A monopoly, the Lottery eventually took in from $20 to $30 million a year from all over the United States. It was carefully rigged to return 40 per cent to franchisers, who paid only $40,000 for a license. There were no taxes.

Major Edward A. Burke was lottery agent for the state, and its political kingpin. He became the Boss of Louisiana, yet no one knew where he came from. Some said he grew up in Illinois. Others said he claimed to have fought for the Confederacy. Burke apparently had never been a soldier, much less a major.

He talked so glibly and maneuvered so slickly, he made the opportunistic carpetbaggers seem clumsy by comparison. Major Burke was in Washington during the 1877 Electoral College crisis. There he was said to have helped secure the bargain for withdrawal of Federal troops. He also was said to have delayed the train carrying Federal soldiers on his company's railroad line in 1874, thus preventing them from halting the White League insurrection. Major Burke was canonized by hearsay and declared a "Redeemer Extraordinary" by Louisiana citizens who elected the swaggering carpetbagger State Treasurer.

The finagling Major bought the *New Orleans Times*. When the *New Orleans Democrat*, chief journalistic enemy of the Lottery, faced bankruptcy, Burke bought that paper, with financial help from "his" Lottery). He then merged the two papers into one resounding voice of Bourbon redemption and Lottery salvation. Burke's power and that of the Louisiana Lottery went unchallenged for 10 years.

Being treasurer had its special rewards. Burke could control and regulate the use of state money, and he did. Up in Atlanta, the *Constitution*'s editor Henry W. Grady was plumping a new catchphrase for Dixie, "The New South." In 1884 Major Burke gobbled it up as rallying cry for his newest brainchild: The World's Industrial and Cotton Centennial Exposition, commemorating the ascendancy of King Cotton in the South. He formed a committee of rich, honorable men, including Edmund Richardson, second largest cotton planter in the world (the Khedive of Egypt ranked first by a few bales).

The Cotton Exposition was a grandiose attempt to revitalize the city's sagging economy, and "bind up the wounds of the Civil War and Reconstruction." When his local citizens' group ran short of funds, Major Burke hustled to Washington and squeezed $1 million from his fellow Democratic "Redeemers."

The Exposition opened, barely beating its deadline, on December 16, 1884. Major Burke boldly predicted it would draw four million people and

Canal and Royal, 1884:
Downtown New Orleans
had electrified its streetcars
but horses still pulled
carriages.

gross $5 million. It wound up drawing only one million and losing $500,000. One reporter termed it "a Colossal White Elephant floundering in a mire of stupidity, mismanagement, and corruption."

Much of the Exposition was impressive, however. The main building was the largest edifice ever constructed, covering 33 acres in Audubon Park. It contained 22 miles of corridors and more elevators than existed in all the rest of the world. There were two large buildings inside the main structure. An exhibition hall seated 8,000 people and a music hall accommodated 11,000. The pipe organ was the largest in North America. The Horticultural Hall was a magnificent observatory built of glass and wood, shaped like a cross and surmounted by a 90-foot tower. The glass tower was illuminated at night and was visible 20 miles away. It housed collections of palms, acacias, and cacti.

The great International Cotton Exposition fell deeply into debt. It almost closed twice before it officially expired in June 1885. On balance, it produced no new industry for New Orleans and very little commerce. It probably caused local businessmen and bankers to avoid any bold future "New South" ventures. But it did improve Southern morale and Northern attitudes after two decades of war and rancor. Its futuristic designs and techniques had a profound impact on architecture. Horticultural Hall remained until it was blown apart by the 1915 hurricane. Today, nothing tangible is left on the site except the site itself, Audubon Park.

The most important contribution of the 1884 Exposition was probably the defrocking of that bogus Confederate Major, Edward A. Burke. He ran again for State Treasurer in 1887. When irregularities developed in his campaign, Burke found it suddenly imperative to travel to London on unspecified business. This allowed state auditors an opportunity to check his records at leisure. They showed a shortage of $1,267,905.

By the time the Major was indicted for embezzlement and forgery, he had settled permanently in Honduras. There, the fugitive from Louisiana courts was treated like an elder statesman. He entertained many distinguished visitors, including Theodore Roosevelt and William McKinley. He chose not to return to the United States but to "redeem" Honduras, where he died.

I rish Channel: They came by the boatload, with little more than what they could carry by hand, fleeing persecution and famine. In the 1850s, they escaped the potato famine only to be wiped out in droves by yellow fever. They were the Irish, and they concentrated in the township of Lafayette, a clannish, self-protective, pugnacious bunch whose Irish Channel was scrupulously avoided by strangers. Aliens usually were greeted "with a shower of bricks."

The term Irish Channel is obscure. One story holds that Irish immigrants sailing upriver were told to look for the "channel marker." When they spotted the elevated light over Noud's emporium of good food and good cheer they'd yell, "there she is, the Irish Channel." Another explanation is more prosaic: whenever it rained in New Orleans, which was often, water poured down from the rich, elevated Garden District onto the poor low-lying Irish in their undrained mud-wallow. It literally became the Irish Channel.

The Garden District was the home of the Anglos, an uptown enclave of wealthy *nouveaux riches*. Its homes were sneeringly called Prairie Palaces by snobbish Creoles. They exhibited a dilettante's taste for mélange: Greek Revival, Italian Villa, Italianate, and Queen Anne style. The Garden District was noted for its distinctively manicured gardens and iron palings. These iron fences were dictated by necessity. Irish roustabouts drove cattle smack through the Garden District, trained bulldogs nipping at their hooves. The snorting beasts stampeded wooden fences and trampled flowerbeds on their way to the slaughterhouses down below in the Channel.

In 1890 New Orleans had only one and a half miles of paved roadway inside its city limits. There were, however, 26 different street car lines with more than 200 miles of track.

There was great prejudice against the Irish in the early days. They were considered radicals, immoral, and carriers of the plague. Like the Germans, they kept to themselves, worked hard, and made their own way. The entire Irish Channel stank of the slaughterhouse, but the Irish laughed it off, grew vegetables in their tiny backyards, and raised goats, pigs, and cows. The legendary Kathleen Hickey was said to keep her horse in the kitchen on chilly winter nights, so he could sleep by the stove.

They were so poor "they ate turkey on Sunday and pigtails the rest of the week." The main diversion for the children was swimming in the gutters after a heavy rain. For adults, wakes were a grand entertainment. The roughest spot in New Orleans was the corner of St. Mary and Religious Streets. Fist fights with the German gang from Little Saxony broke out there.

For many years, it was unsafe to enter the Channel after dark. Certain places, such as the Bucket of Blood, were hangouts for legendary toughs like Rat Tooth Flynn and the Crowbar Gang. Toughest of all was the St. Mary's Market Gang which terrorized the local public market, warranted doubling of the police (mostly Irish), and probably killed a black officer in 1892.

Sometimes, Irish gangs visited the Garden District and tore up shrubbery or smashed fences and benches. Sometimes, at night, poor Irish boys would sneak up and peek in the windows, and gawk at the shimmering chandeliers, bright crystal, oil paintings, fancy butlers, and maids. One prominent Irish public official confessed his burning ambition was kindled the night he "peeked in" on an unsuspecting Anglo family banqueting "like Lords . . . looking like some great old English Christmas card."

Matrangas and Provenzanos: The self-serving Redeemers were overthrown in the New Orleans election of 1888 when a reform group patterned after the White League surrounded the polls with riflemen. This indelicate show of force kept hoodlums from intimidating voters. Backed by the Young Men's Democratic Association, the newly elected mayor came equipped with a surname to reckon with, Joseph Shakespeare.

Dripping integrity, Shakespeare pared the budget, fired deadheads, and reorganized the police force. He appointed 31-year-old David C. Hennessy as his chief. Hennessy was the son of a policeman who was murdered in a St. Ann street coffee-house. His brother Mike, a private detective, was killed in 1886 by a paid assassin who journeyed from New Orleans to Galveston to execute him. Almost from the day of his appointment, David Hennessy was a marked man.

The Mafia came to New Orleans about 1878 and soon flourished. Two rival factions, the Matrangas and Provenzanos, declared open war over control of the riverfront banana wharves. The vendetta led to a half dozen killings before Chief Hennessy agreed to testify against the Matrangas in a pending lawsuit. Two nights before he was to appear in court, Hennessy was shot dead on Basin Street near Girod.

The Mafia's murder society, the Stoppagherra, was suspected. Twenty-one members of the Matranga family were arrested and 19 indicted, 11 of them named principals in the assassination of David Hennessy. The evidence seemed conclusive, but the jury acquitted six men and said it could not agree on another three. When accusations of jury tampering surfaced, the public was outraged. A group of the city's prominent citizens met, led by attorney W. S. Parkerson. They issued a memorable declaration: "When the machinery of justice breaks down, the power to try and to execute criminals reverts to the people." On March 14, 1891, vigilantes broke into the parish prison, sought out members of the Matranga gang and summarily executed them— nine were shot and two were hanged.

Mayor Shakespeare deplored "the necessity" of killing the prisoners, but "the Italians had taken the law into their own hands and we had to do the same." Dozens of businesses and commercial groups, including the Board of Trade and the Cotton Exchange, publicly endorsed the lynching. To avoid an international incident, the United States government expressed regrets to

Italy and paid an indemnity of $25,000. Later, it was officially reported that Mafiosi had carried out the Hennessy assassination, although some historians strongly dispute this conclusion. In any case, law-abiding citizens of Italian extraction suffered from the stigma brought on by Mafia activity.

The Black Hand Society resorted to kidnapping and the crudest blackmail against prominent members of the Italian community. In 1907, the body of 8-year-old Walter Lamana, son of an Italian undertaker, was found floating in a swamp. Italian leaders formed the Italian Vigilance Committee to reinforce the police. Six people were apprehended and convicted, and the Black Hand virtually disappeared from the area.

By 1910, so many Italian immigrants had arrived in New Orleans that they represented almost one-third of the population. Most came from Sicily where the soil was poor and absentee landlords ruled with feudal disdain. Arriving in New Orleans by the boatload, they set up small farms, groceries, and markets. Ten thousand settled around Kenner's "Green Gold" fields, growing cabbage, shallots, turnips, beets, garlic, hot peppers, string beans. Sicilians introduced the eggplant, and developed superior strawberries and tomatoes. Every night, a procession of wagons rumbled into New Orleans bound for the French Market with fresh produce. Italians like Giuseppe Uddo, founder of Progresso Foods, soon dominated the French Market.

In time, the French Quarter was known as Little Italy. The new arrivals found living space in the dilapidated houses of the Vieux Carré. The architecture was comfortably Mediterranean and they were close to their businesses. A few old Creole families occupied ancestral homes, but most had either died off or moved out to the Creole faubourgs. Huge Italian families crowded into small houses and apartments, bringing goats and chickens, provoking slurs from other ethnic groups which felt the economic competition.

German immigrants were more likely to have education and skills. A new wave arrived during the German political turmoil of the 1840s, bringing bakers, brewers, metal workers, shoemakers, as well as some doctors, lawyers, and teachers. They settled in Carrollton and Lafayette, across the river in Algiers, and in that part of Faubourg Marigny known as Little Saxony. Between 1820 and 1860, an estimated 30,000 arrived in New Orleans.

Louisiana Lottery: The great hall at the corner of St. Charles and Union Street was crowded with nervous clients. At one end of the room was a raised platform on which rested two large glass wheels. In one wheel were brass tubes, containing 10,000 tiny tickets. The other was the receptacle for the few hundred tubes inside of which the prizes were

The Italian Quarter, 1906: The French moved out of the French Quarter and the Italians moved in. Here, Madison Street.

P.G.T. Beauregard was one of the few Confederate generals who adapted to the New South. He refused to attend Jefferson Davis' funeral because he "didn't like him." Much criticized for stooping to make money, he left a goodly estate when he died in 1893.

listed. Two blindfolded boys from a local orphanage would make the drawings.

At precisely two minutes before the hour, General Jubal Early, hero of the Confederacy, entered. He stood beside one wheel, attired in Confederate gray. The drama heightened as a small, ramrod-straight Creole followed Early into the hall, precisely one minute before the hour. It was General P.G.T. Beauregard, shill for the Louisiana Lottery. He reportedly received $30,000 a year for working about one hour a week.

The Louisiana Lottery, or Golden Octopus, was the brainchild of a New York syndicate operator, Charles T. Howard, who had moved to New Orleans in 1852. A burly, bluff, fast-talking man, Howard claimed to have been a Confederate officer in both the Army and the Navy. He was realistic in his appraisal of gambling, however. Orleanians loved it. Churches and schools had conducted lotteries since colonial days.

A Short History of New Orleans

The carpetbag legislature of 1868 was hungry to license gambling, provided there was a proper incentive. Howard spread around a reported $300,000 and the solons licensed the Louisiana Lottery for 25 years as tax-free monopoly, obligated only to pay the state $40,000 for support of Charity Hospital. To set the proper tone, it began with a demonstration of fiscal sleight-of-hand.

The syndicate's only financial requirement was that it show one-tenth of the capital stock of $1 million. The promoters borrowed $100,000, deposited it in a bank for one day, withdrew it, and paid off the loan. The Golden Octopus thus began with no capital at all; it did have a slush fund of $15,000 to "calm" legislators.

What they created was undoubtedly the largest gambling organization ever to exist in the United States before the twentieth century. At the height of its powers, the Lottery's gross income was $29 million, less than 60 percent of which was given out in prizes. For over 20 years, it dominated the political, social, and economic life of New Orleans. The Octopus wrapped its tentacles around the state legislature in 1868, and smothered it effectively for 22 years; it controlled every newspaper in New Orleans, and most others in the state. Since it was the biggest business in town, it allied itself with the city's four major banks—and it controlled them, too.

The Lottery was a money machine, pure and simple. It spent part of its huge revenue "buying" support. It subsidized political campaigns and purchased votes. It contributed to education and sanitation and orphans' homes. Anytime there was need—a family flooded out, a destitute widow, a family on the verge of starving—the Lottery was there, with its benevolent tentacles, embracing everyone.

The Lottery financed the French Opera House, the construction of cotton mills, and sugar refineries. Everybody in New Orleans bought tickets—rich, poor, indigent, desperate—and yet eventually 90 percent of the Lottery's business was out of state. Monthly sales in Chicago topped $85,000.

There were daily, semi-monthly, and semi-annual drawings. The Grand Prize was listed at $600,000, but no one ever won it. A New Orleans barber won $300,000 on a $20 ticket. A Chicago policeman cashed a $15,000 ticket and bought a saloon, which he named Louisiana. Lottery number books, Fortune books, Dream books, and Lucky books were peddled everywhere, and a folklore of hunches developed. A dream of a dead woman with gray hair meant play 49. A naked female leg belonging neither to your wife nor mistress meant number 11. Lottery hawkers displayed trained parakeets who, for 5¢, could pick you a winner.

Governor Nicholls vetoed renewal of the Lottery charter in 1890, saying:

"I can not permit my right hand to sign away what I gave my left hand to preserve: the honor of my state." The nonplussed legislature resolved that the governor had no right to veto an amendment and adjourned.

The Federal government chopped off the Golden Octopus' tentacles. Half the mail arriving in New Orleans was Lottery mail. Lottery offices were located in a half dozen big cities. Congress passed a law forbidding the sending of tickets through the mails, and closed the mails to newspapers which contained lottery ads.

The Louisiana Lottery was disbanded in 1907, after operating in exile out of Honduras for eight years, through it continued illegally until World War II.

Storyville and Jazz: There was nothing in the Western Hemisphere like the 38 blocks of legitimized sin called Storyville. It was named after Alderman Sidney Story who, in January 1897, sponsored the ordinance creating a special area adjacent to the French Quarter in which prostitution not only flourished but was the principal business.

Thirty-five mansions, three and four stories high, adorned lower Basin Street, Storyville's main drag. The madams were imperious dowager-vixens who presided over crews of 15 to 20 women of various races and temperament. Storyville's side streets were populated with hundreds of "quick tricks" and parlor houses, staffed by two or three girls each. Then there were the long rows of "cribs," each about seven feet wide by ten feet deep, big enough for a bed, a chair and a window, out of which the hookers leaned, peddling themselves.

The Queen of Storyville was Lulu White. A black woman, she ran Mahogany Hall, the most elegant brothel in town. Lulu was bulky, brassy, vulgar, with an ill-fitting wig the color of a clown's. She wore diamonds everywhere: on her neck, ears, hair, fingers, arms, even in her mouth—she had a special diamond-encrusted bridge made to assure a dazzling smile. Mahogany Hall matched her taste. It was mainly mahogany, shined to mirror gloss, with marble polished to satisfy a Medici. There were oriental carpets, gilded mirrors, crystal chandeliers, five parlors, and 15 bedrooms. There were also entertainers playing something that, for some reason, they called "jass."'

The King of Storyville was a former accountant named Tom Anderson, who ran the Fair Play Saloon at the corner of Basin and Iberville. It was the first saloon in town to use electric lights. One hundred bulbs lit up the interior, while outside a huge electric sign spelled out his name. The bar was mahogany, half a block long, and the floors were tile. Upstairs, Anderson ran a whorehouse.

Storyville became "Anderson County" before long, a "must" stop for celebrities, even Carrie Nation. Anderson set up hot milk for her while she

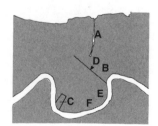

A. "Wishing Spot" (Voodoo ceremonies)
B. Storyville
C. Audubon Park (1884 Expo)
D. Canal St.
E. Irish Channel
F. Garden District

A Short History of New Orleans

ranted about the evils of demon rum, until a Storyville policeman, pledged to keep law and order, gently led her away. In Anderson County, Tom Anderson was the Law. He controlled over a dozen bagnios and bars, adjudicated arguments, and had his pick both of madams and "ladies." The Mayor of Storyville even ran for the state legislature, won, and served eight years.

Next door to Anderson's saloon was Josie Arlington's four-storied mansion at 225 Basin street, with its gaudy Hall of Mirrors and Japanese, Turkish, and Viennese parlors. The Blue Book, Storyville's illustrated magazine, called it "absolutely and unquestionably the most decorative and costly fitted out sporting palace ever placed before the American public." Josie employed a black piano player called "The Professor" and served only imported champagne at $50 a bottle.

Anything sexually weird was called Parisian in those days. A tough bisexual exhibitionist named Emma Johnson was named the Parisian Queen of America by the Blue Book, a combination Police Gazette and Sears Roebuck Catalog of the Flesh, with personalized advertisements and chatty bits of Storyville gossip. Antonia Gonzales advertised "first-class octoroons" and boasted of being "the only Singer of Opera and Female Cornetist" in Storyville. The 25¢ Blue Book contained a complete list of all prostitutes in residence, black and white, and a list of "Late Arrivals." At the district's peak, there were 250 houses and about 2,000 prostitutes, including all the "crib" girls and two- and three-girl operations. The magazine's front and middle portions featured regular ads for saloons, lawyers, cabarets, liquor-dealers, restaurants, and breweries. The last 15 to 20 pages were devoted to more exotic ads: "Chiquita the Spanish Beauty" or "two Orientals, very exotic, just arrived."

Storyville ran full blast for 20 years under the shelter of the law. It was successful because, from the beginning, public opinion favored the existence of such a district.

It was tawdry, lurid, sinful—but at far remove the names have a certain glow: Martha Clark and her select stable of two, Big Casino and Little Casino; Willie O. Berrera, who smoked cigars and was her own bouncer; Queen Emmette, known as Diamond Tooth; and Josephine Ice Box, so cool the house paid a prize to any who unfroze her (no one ever did); the black madam called Minnie Ha-Ha who claimed to be an Indian Princess; and Mary Thompson who once had a runaway virgin arrested "for stealing herself."

People like Spanish Agnes were not so funny. She ran an Employment Agency as a front for her real business: entrapping young maidens into the "sporting life." Goggle-eyed tourists were propagandized with a "Guide to Fast Women," "Streetwalking Tarts," and "Tips to Avoid Holdups." The idea

Call me madam: Lulu White, the Queen of Storyville, and her . . . employees.

was to patronize "class joints" where you were—relatively—safe.

Only 20 years after its founding, Storyville's gilded facade was moldering. Its end came with World War I when the Navy Department ordered all prostitution halted within five miles of a naval base. On November 13, 1917, Storyville became an instant ghost town.

Storyville's end came with World War I when the Navy Department ordered all prostitution halted within five miles of a naval base. On November 13, 1917, Storyville became an instant ghost town.

By the 1920s, mores had changed, including attitudes toward premarital sex. Even Creoles were cuddling while courting. Countess Willie Piazza, the celebrated intellectual madam, observed: "The country club girls are ruining my business." Then she took down the faded motto on the wall of her deserted bordello. It read: "It takes a heap of loving to make a home a house."

Countess Willie made a special contribution to Storyville lore. She spoke seven languages, wore a monocle, and haughtily punctuated her speech with a foot-long cigarette holder. An octoroon, she ran an intellectual and political bordello wherein the Honduran Revolution of 1910 was plotted. One night, she shot a customer dead when he abused one of her girls. She took her motto seriously and shepherded her ladies to every big event, racetrack opera, Sunday mass.

Willie Piazza also knew good music. She employed a brilliant and garrulous piano player who told everybody one night he invented ragtime, and the next night, jazz. His name was Jelly Roll Morton. Later, the lesser known Tony Jackson made the ivories dance. Jazz was not born in Storyville, but it was incubated in those bawdy house parlors.

The word "jazz" has an uncertain origin, but may derive from the West African Mandingo word *jasi*—"to act out of the ordinary." Al Rose of the New Orleans Jazz Museum says jazz is basically "any music played in two/four or four/four syncopated time by two or more tonal instruments improvising collectively."

Jazz was not invented. It "happened"—at parades and funerals, in black churches and octoroon balls, at band concerts and barbecues, in backrooms and bordellos. Buddy Bolden went to church each Sunday and reinforced what he heard with the rhythms of the street—for street cries filled the air. African "answering chants," first heard in Congo Square Voodoo dances, made their way into the music, with instruments parodying voices, trumpets taking the lead. White music, too, was an influence, for plantation work songs and gospel hymns were richly orchestrated after exposure to more formal European or classical music.

Years before anyone even used the word "jazz," brass bands marched through New Orleans streets, breeding public rhythms. These were picked up and reinforced by the many Carnival parades, always with the emphasis on "brass" and the big beat. Early Dixieland picked up that martial beat and wove it into tricky, syncopated patterns. As early as 1838, the *Picayune* described New Orleans' love of parades and of "brass," calling it a "real mania." With all the city's nationalities, there were holiday parades every other week or else militia, fire department, or secret lodge parades.

The final amalgam in the creation of jazz may have come with Jim Crow, around 1890. Strict segregation broke down color lines within the black community, forcing light-skinned blacks to accept their darker brethren. The musicianship of the black elite was mixed with the freed slave's passion and feeling.

But Louis Armstrong said it best: "Man, if you have to explain it, it ain't jazz." His life story is almost tantamount to the history of jazz. Born July 4, 1900, he began wandering French Quarter streets at the age of six, singing and dancing for pennies. New Year's Day, 1913, Louie found a pistol at home and accidentally shot it off. They sent him to the Waif's Home for correction and, as it turned out, for his musical education.

The social highlight of each day at the Waif's Home was the raising and lowering the flag, accompanied by bugle calls. Louis, who had never played the trumpet, got the job and America was richer for it. Along the line he was a milkman, ragman, coal man, and (after King Oliver took him in) a trumpet man. He played the riverboats and pleasure palaces of New Orleans and then took his jazz up river to Chicago.

Satchmo was loved the world over; he once had to wear a catcher's mask during a South American parade to protect his million-dollar lips from friendly abuse. He was so popular that mail reached him addressed simply "Louis Armstrong, Mr. Jazz, U.S.A." When the Russians flocked to hear him, Louis slyly observed: "It seems to me they ain't havin' so many wars since I been blowin' over there." Asked if the Russians understood jazz, Louis smiled and answered: "Pops, sometimes I don't understand it myself."

It was a group of white New Orleans musicians that performed the real missionary work. In 1914 they formed the Original Dixieland Jass Band. With Nick LaRocca in the lead, they recorded several lively tunes in a strange, syncopated cadence unknown to the New Yorkers listening at the Victor Talking Machine Company in New York. The first jass record was called Livery Stable Blues, complete with imitated whinnies and chicken cackles. Actually, it was a jazzed up version of an old hymn, "The Holy City." It was a phenomenal success.

Then the trouble began. Yellow Nunez, a former band member, claimed

Satchmo: Louis Armstrong carried his trumpet up the river and into musical history. When this photo was taken he was playing with King Oliver and his Creole Jazz Band.

Almost all the early jazz greats were New Orleans musicians; Buddy Bolden, King Oliver, Jelly Roll Morton, Bunk Johnson, Kid Ory, Sidney Bechet, and Louis Armstrong are only a few. They played for social events at Perseverance Hall, Economy Hall, and Funky Butt Hall, as well as the more palatial mansions of Storyville.

he wrote the tune. Nick LaRocca said that was impossible. The judge ruled that nobody wrote the tune . . . because it was "an unmusical noise."

The furor over rock 'n roll a half-century later was mild compared to the moral indignation over jazz. In 1918, a New Orleans critic wrote: "Jazz is a manifestation of a low streak in man's taste. Although New Orleans has been called its birthplace . . . we do not recognize parenthood." Even so, the Original Dixieland Jass Band was an international sensation within two years. They played the Palace of Dance in London in 1919. British critics said their music was "a musical joke hardly worth attempting." Nick LaRocca sadly remained a prophet without honor in his own hometown, but his records established the new musical form throughout the world.

Yellow Jack and Swampbeaters: The city's first water works was established in 1810. Its primitive pipes were made of hollow cypress logs. Slave labor pumped water from the river into a reservoir, then distributed it by cart. The water was brown and untreated. Most people eschewed it in favor of rain water from cisterns. By 1900, there were 68,000 homes in New Orleans, and as many cisterns.

A water system using iron pipes was built in 1833 but it broke down. After the Civil War, the city bought the water works system and almost went bankrupt trying to run it. Finally, a Sewerage and Water Board was formed in 1893. By the turn of the century it had developed a plan that would cost $27.5 million. They proposed to drain the city and eliminate once and for all the network of filthy, disease-breeding, open gutters that had made New Orleans the nation's unhealthiest city.

New Orleans was an isolated city in 1905, cut off from fearful neighboring communities. Many towns would not receive mail from New Orleans unless it was fumigated. Before the epidemic the city's health officer, Dr. Quitman Kohnke, scoffed at a mosquito eradication plan as "just another fad."

Before the swamp was beaten, though, it took one last shot. On July 21, 1905, the Board of Health announced yellow fever was loose again. There was panic at first. Tens of thousands fled the city. Most knew that Walter Reed had proven the *Aedes aegypti* mosquito was the disease's carrier, and that it bred indiscriminately in their open cisterns and filthy gutters. They had known it for five years, and yet few cisterns were screened.

Suddenly, a wonderful thing happened. Panic turned into resolution. Medical officials, health agenices, and citizen groups were coordinated in a city-wide scouring. Sixty-eight thousand cisterns were screened and oiled. Seven hundred fifty-three miles of open gutters and drains were salted. Despite a month's head start, Bronze John was stopped cold. In a city of 325,000 (where Yellow Jack had claimed 10,000 just 50 years before), only 452 people died. There were no cannons to "break up the miasma" or stinking "tarpots" to smother the air, just resolution. Never again was there an epidemic of yellow fever in New Orleans. Most cisterns were taken down by 1920.

The man who finally conquered the swamp was Albert Baldwin Wood, an electrical engineer for the Sewerage and Water Board. Wood invented 12-foot screw pumps of such power they pulled 10 million cubic feet of water (about 320 million tons) out of the "soup bowl" of New Orleans every year. This engineering feat so impressed the Dutch they used Wood's pumps to drain the Zuider Zee.

Wood's system, completed in 1914, drained the "floating land" of its excess subsurface moisture. Six feet below sea level, the city was literally underlaced with a network of piping, more than 120 miles of subterranean canals. Eight pumping stations, using Wood's machines, battled the city's 64 inches of annual rainfall with such authority they could empty Lake Pontchartrain in three days. All that underground piping, if stretched end to end, would wind up in Seattle, Washington. Drinking water soon was pumped through 125 miles of arteries, devoid of impurities.

A property tax was proposed to cover the cost of fresh water. Creoles objected: "We pay to install this plumbing, why pay again just to flush it?" They forced an amendment providing free water for toilet flushing (200 gallons a month).

Twilight of the Creoles: Out of fierce pride, inborn arrogance, dislike of Americans, and an aversion to hard work, the Creoles gradually cut themselves out of an effective partnership in New Orleans' future. Their fall from grace was incomprehensible to old Creoles brought up to believe in the uniqueness of their station, and of themselves as *sortis de la cuisse de Jupiter* (sprung from the thigh of Jupiter).

The Creole code was firm and, ultimately, strangulating. Creoles rarely worked at trades, or as merchants. Physical labor was left to the blacks. Creoles were planters, bankers, and cotton brokers. Ambition was stunted, opportunity limited. In the end, many Creoles were economically crushed.

Creole women devoted their entire lives to the one province where they were allowed freedom—the home. They were skilled dancers, conversationalists, loving mothers, and extraordinary cooks. They married strictly by arrangement, were loyal to their husbands, and were expected to produce a horde of children.

Courtships were severely confined; a Creole maiden was never allowed to be alone with a beau. A formal marriage contract was drawn up, listing property, furniture, cash, and slaves. The honeymoon was spent in the home of the bride, and the newlyweds did not leave their room for five days. They might not appear on the street for two weeks. After that, the entire family was virtually as one. The Creole *famille* was the absolute center of the universe.

There was an art to everything in life and, to the Creole, cooking was the ultimate art. No greater epicures ever lived than the *crème de la crème* of New

End of an era: The center of the Creoles' universe, the French Opera House, was gutted by fire in 1919.

Orleans.

If the family was center of its universe, then the French Opera House was both its moon and sun. During Mardi Gras, it was constantly awhirl with activity. Americans were astonished to see tiny, frail Creole ladies dance four nights a week at balls. In the loges at the opera there were special screened boxes for pregnant ladies, people in mourning, and women of questionable virtue.

Creole families were so large that when everyone started talking it was called a "Gumbo Ya-ya." Half a dozen at least would be named Marie, so the Creoles assigned pet names: Cheri Bébé, Tounoute, Nounouse, Doudouce, Bouboutse. The family included quantities of aunts and cousins, grandmothers and grandfathers, and even *fainéants* (loafers) who were dutifully

A Short History of New Orleans

supported. One Parisian who married a Creole girl said he didn't marry a woman, he married 510 relatives.

Creole women used no cosmetics. (American women said their makeup was "extremely artful.") A Creole woman was judged by the milky whiteness of her skin. She wore veils whenever she went outdoors. Not only was suntan disgraceful, it started rumors that she was *café au lait*.

Old Creole songs were obsessed with two things: food and eating, and black women attempting to pass as white. The most famous, "Toucoutou," concerns the competition between a white wife and her husband's quadroon mistress. Each verse ends with the same refrain: "There is no soap strong enough to whiten your skin." "Mo Che Cousin" is an epic 100 verses, all dealing with either food or mulattoes "passing." "Dame Tartina" is a gustatory classic. Only a Creole could invent a lyric comparing a woman, limb by limb, with various foods. Dame Tartina, it seems, is "made like a sandwich." She has a "nose of marzipan," "ears of cracknel," "shoes of chocolate," "stocking of honey," and much more.

Creoles thought of themselves as French, and called themselves French until the late 1800s. They imported French wines, French books, French clothes, and French furniture. Their children were often educated in Paris. They liked themselves so much they felt there could be no improvement. When, on a rare occasion, an Irishman or a German married into the *crème de la crème*, they were quietly absorbed. O'Brien became Obreon. Zweig became LaBranche. The Creole seal was stamped on everything—Creole cooking, Creole taste, Creole cabbages, Creole tomatoes, Creole gumbo, Creole horses. Almost everything they owned or prized was given a special French name.

So circumscribed was the Creole universe that their grand hyperbole was "as big as *les Quatre Paroisses*" (the Four Parishes—Orleans, Jefferson, St. Bernard, St. Tammany), as "big as the whole world."

Many historians believe the Civil War was the beginning of the end for this haughty, inbred people. Quite probably, the Creoles were doomed once the Americans captured political control about 1840.

The French language began losing its dominance and the fiercely French Creoles saw their children become Americanized, too. Deprived of their legacy, the *crème de la crème* even retreated from the French Quarter, leaving it a shabby relic for years. The proud Pontalbas became tenements, clotheslines strung out across once-handsome galleries. An immigrant family kept a cow on the second floor and chickens ran everywhere. The Vieux Carré became a slum. The Merchants Exchange, built for $100,000 in 1836, was a flophouse, a refuge for rats and panhandlers. All that was left was the old French Opera House, and that reminder of grander days burned down on the night of February 4, 1919.

The Changing Crescent

8

"Politics in Louisiana," Huey Long said, "is the sport of kings." And until the "Kingfish" came along, most Louisianians were mere spectators. Huey changed the rules. A product of an impoverished rural section in the northern part of the state, he gave the poor, ill-educated, disenfranchised majority the vote, and delivered on just enough promises to win their undying devotion. In the words of one critic, "all he asked in return was that they surrender their civil rights."

Huey Long led a poor white rebellion in Louisiana. It altered politics almost overnight, and brought a deceptive first taste of democracy to a citizenry that had known mostly aristocratic, one-party rule. Both blacks and poor whites had been manipulated shamelessly and state government was dominated by corporations such as Standard Oil.

Huey's populist dream was spawned in Winn County, a cantankerous enclave that voted against secession in 1861 and for Eugene Debs in 1920. After flying through an eight-month law course at Tulane, Long passed the bar, and "came out running for office." He used the State Public Service Commission as his springboard and Standard Oil was his whipping boy. Oil was the new element in Louisiana politics, a huge new object of taxation and regulation which, properly managed, might also prove a benefit to the common folk.

"Hit the Big Boy" was Long's credo, and he lashed out recklessly. Governor John Parker sued him for libel, following a Long broadside accusing Standard Oil of running the state from 226 Broadway in New York. Huey escaped with a $1 fine. In 1923, on his first day of eligibility—his 30th birthday—Huey Long filed as candidate for governor. He ran third, polling an impressive 74,000 votes, despite rains that kept many of his poor white con-

Opposite page
The Crescent today: Bienville's beautiful crescent (viewed from a point uptown) is still there, but highrises occupy the Poydras Street corridor—once called The Swamp.

stituency mired on back roads.

Long's Pulitzer Prize-winning biographer, T. Harry Williams, called him the first realist in Southern politics, the first to address himself to basic needs. His program was carefully tailored to redress old grievances. There were only 300 miles of paved roads in Louisiana. Louisiana had the highest illiteracy rate in the United States. Louisiana textbooks were antiquated and worn out. There was no bridge across the Mississippi River. Long promised more roads, better schools, free textbooks, and two new bridges.

Huey Long was elected governor in 1928, and 20,000 poor whites came rumbling into Baton Rouge, by truck, auto, horse and wagon. Dr. Joe Gray Taylor calls it "the watershed of Louisiana history," a complete transfer of power. Long put an end to government by "gentlemen" who, even when they were honest were only concerned with preserving their own position, status, and wealth.

When Long pushed for an extra tax on Standard Oil, he was impeached. Two days of frenzied wheeling and dealing bought the support of 15 legislators, enough to forestall conviction. "I buy 'em like sacks of potatoes," Huey said, referring to the solons. He added a prophetic statement: "I used to try persuasion and reason and logic. From now on I'm a dynamiter. I dynamite 'em out of my way."

The Kingfish published his own newspaper, the *American Progress*, wrote a book, *Every Man a King*, offering a program to end the Depression, co-authored his own theme song of the same title, and published a futuristic fantasy called *My First Days in the White House*. "I've got just the job for you, Frank," Huey tells the vanquished Franklin D. Roosevelt in the fantasy, "Secretary of the Navy—you have the experience."

In 1932, this profane prophet of Utopia became a U.S. Senator, manipulating the state by long distance through a handpicked stooge, Governor O. K. Allen. His demagogic Share the Wealth campaign, a pastiche of vague nostrums, attracted a purported 2 million adherents. Fearful of assassination, he was surrounded by a phalanx of beefy bodyguards toting .45s.

The final weeks of his life were devoted to an exercise in democratic subversion. Long sardonically declared "Partial Martial Law" and sent out trucks full of National Guardsmen to "protect" polling places. He hustled back to Baton Rouge and jammed through a series of "dictatorship laws" that effectively stripped Louisiana's parishes and cities, including New Orleans, of local self-government.

On September 7, 1935, Carl Austin Weiss, Jr., a thin, bespectacled man in a white linen suit, son-in-law of Judge Benjamin Pavy, whom Long had gerrymandered from office, stepped from behind a capitol pillar and shot

Huey Long. The assassin was shredded by at least 26 bullets. Long was taken to Lady of the Lake Hospital. There was an inexplicable delay before he went to surgery. Two New Orleans surgeons summoned to Baton Rouge supposedly "met with an accident" and turned back. Too late, Dr. Arthur Vidrine attempted an operation. Long was dead. That was the final irony of Huey Long's war on all who opposed him. Disdaining the New Orleans medical establishment, the Kingfish had named a country doctor to head the mammoth Charity Hospital. The city's sophisticated medics were aghast; Vidrine, they said, was incompetent.

New Orleans and Louisiana were unalterably changed by Huey Long's poor white revolution. Politics were restructured for the next 35 years. Instead of a genuine two-party system, a contest between Longs and anti-Longs developed. The state was cut along the "bias" — northern versus southern Louisiana, rural versus urban (New Orleans), Protestant versus Catholic.

"God help Loozyana if I die," Huey once said, "my rascals will steal the state blind." Even before his open coffin went on public display in the capitol rotunda and 100,000 mourners passed for a final view, his courtiers were in chaos. With no successors, only stooges, a half dozen self-appointed Kingfishermen scrambled to occupy the throne. Judge Richard Leche, an affable sybarite with a taste for the good life, was anointed to run for governor. Huey's bellicose younger brother, Earl, custodian of the magic Long name, ran for lieutenant governor.

The Leche-Long ticket polled more votes than anyone, including Huey, in Louisiana history. In New Orleans Mayor Semmes "Turkey Neck" Walmsley, Long's uptown nemesis, resigned two years before his term expired. Walsmley reluctantly agreed to leave office on the condition that Governor-Elect Leche restore to New Orleans some of the powers the Kingfish had stripped. It was a deal born of desperation and it paved the way for a brazen political coup.

The Kingfish at rest: Huey Long's long hooey ended with his assassination.

Huey Long used political ridicule like an artist. The Mayor of New Orleans was always "Turkey Neck" Walmsley. Another opponent was "Kinky" Howard, an insinuation that he had mixed blood. The only man who ever beat the Kingfish at his own game was Harold Ickes. "Huey Long," he said, "has halitosis of the intellect."

Louisiana Hayride: Rarely, if ever, has an American mayor served six years without being elected. Robert Maestri of New Orleans did. Maestri, a shrewd, almost inarticulate real estate operator, was head of the State Conservation Committee. The Democrats nominated him, without opposition, to fill Walmsley's unexpired term. There was no primary. There was no election. There was no opposition whatsoever. Maestri had been a principal financial backer and adviser to Huey Long. He knew where the money, the votes, and the bodies were buried.

On August 17, 1936, Maestri became Mayor. Newly-elected Governor Leche promptly rushed through a Constitutional Amendment, never submitted to the voters, extending Maestri's term to six years. Then the captive legislature pushed through a bill that effectively gave Maestri control of the city council and all patronage in New Orleans.

The city was bankrupt. The laconic Maestri, pathetic on a podium, was described by historian Edward F. Haas as "earthy" and a "financial wizard." In two years he had the city on a cash-and-carry basis. In 1942, he finally submitted himself to the voters. It was no contest. Maestri, armed with an overwhelming mandate, consolidated the Long and the Old Regular forces.

According to Louisiana folklore, Mayor Maestri once entertained President Franklin D. Roosevelt at a luncheon featuring Oysters Rockefeller at Antoine's. Afterwards, Maestri inquired: "How ya' like dem ersters, Chief?"

Meanwhile, the state as a whole was taken on what came to be known as the "Louisiana Hayride." One historian called it the "most systematic theft upon an American State" ever undertaken. Huey Long's "rascals" set the stage when they made political peace with the Roosevelt administration. Federal money, reduced to a trickle before Huey's death, suddenly poured in.

Governor Leche jauntily proclaimed: "When I took the oath of office, I didn't take any vow of poverty." It was the ideal keynote for his term in office, sometimes called "The Second Louisiana Purchase." Leche had baronial tastes. Opponents referred to him as "the governor with the $250,000 home on the $7,500 salary." Besides Governor Leche, the list of high-level finaglers included Dr. James Monroe Smith, president of Louisiana State University, Seymour Weiss, president of the renowned Roosevelt Hotel, prominent contractor Monte Hart, and a dozen others. In 1939, they were buried under a blizzard of indictments, pegged to charges of mail fraud and income tax evasion. Four committed suicide. Seven went to jail, including Leche and Smith.

When Governor Leche was convicted and sentenced to 10 years in Atlanta prison, he refused to feel sorry for himself, or anybody else. "What the hell," he said, "it's an occupational hazard."

Phantom vote counts were common in St. Bernard and Plaquemines Parishes. Dudley Le Blanc, the Cajun flim-flam man who parlayed a patent medicine called Hadacol into $18 million, lost a bid for Governor in 1932. His arch-enemy, Leander Perez, "voted vacant lots and cemeteries, living people twice, and dead people once." Le Blanc received two votes in Plaquemines Parish.

During their heyday, Huey's "rascals" developed astounding schemes to bleed the state. They sold the same downtown hotel, the Bienville, twice to themselves. They systematically tapped Levee Board funds, diverting them into private investments. They used LSU and state materials, vehicles, and personnel to build homes, buildings, garages, driveways. Double-dipping, phantom payrolls, even phantom buildings were among the many refinements developed by the governor and his statehouse gang.

Joachim O. "Bathtub Joe" Fernandez had ridden Huey Long's coattails into Washington as a Congressman, clinching victory with a 2,702-7 margin in St. Bernard Parish (where votes sometimes exceeded the number of registered voters). Unseated after six years in Congress, he resurfaced as a "reformer" in the mayoralty election of 1946. Five days before the qualifying deadline, Fernandez conveniently withdrew from the race and threw his support to Bob Maestri, who was suddenly unopposed. Maestri, who had become mayor without an election 10 years earlier, would be handed a walkover—unless a minor miracle occurred in the next hundred hours.

The Morrison Years: It was not a miracle; it was more like a happy accident. Colonel de Lesseps Story "Chep" Morrison, handsome, articulate scion of a prominent old family, was freshly returned from overseas, the perfect hero for postwar New Orleans to hang its hopes on. Morrison had been elected to the state legislature before serving in the Army in Europe. Re-elected in absentia, a small American flag flew on his unoccupied desk at the state capitol.

Wearing his Army uniform, "Blue Boy" (as friends mischievously called him) announced for mayor, and steadily picked up strength with his vow "to sweep the city clean." The complacent Maestri forces were swept away in the primary and Chep Morrison began his first of four progressive terms as Mayor of New Orleans. The impact of this stunning upset was not lost on Morrison. He told reporters: "The two most surprised people in New Orleans are Bob Maestri and Chep Morrison."

For 16 years, Morrison battled to move the city forward, break upstate control of its destiny, and re-establish home rule. He was thwarted time and again by Huey Long's hebephrenic brother, "Uncle Earl." Earl Long and the "regulars" ganged up to rewrite New Orleans' city charter, gerrymandering a seven-district council they thought they could control. The gerrymander swallowed its own tail. Six Morrison candidates rode a wave of local indignation into office. In effect Earl Long created a new and potent political force: Morrison's Crescent City Democratic Association. It was Long's major political nemesis for 12 years.

Chep Morrison built a solid record, effecting long overdue city improvements. He constructed a series of overpasses and underpasses that eliminated hazardous railway and vehicular crossings. A large central slum area was cleared and replaced by the current city, state, and federal building complex on Loyola Avenue, including the present 11-story City Hall.

Adroit politicking by Morrison and his respected legislative floor leader, Bob Ainsworth (later a federal judge), overcame upstate bickering long enough to push the 24-mile Lake Pontchartrain Causeway, the longest bridge in the world, across the lake in 1956. In 1958, the Greater New Orleans Bridge reached out from downtown New Orleans and gathered in Algiers.

Earl Long was swamp-fox smart. Running for governor against Hale Boggs, Morrison's law-partner, he told his rural audience: "Mr. Boggs has been accused of being a communist. That's hogwash. Mr. Boggs is no communist. He is a Roman Catholic, a dee-vout Roman Cathlic." In North Louisiana, that was enough said.

In 1969 the Second Lake Pontchartrain Causeway became the world's longest bridge. At 126,055 feet, it is 228 feet longer than the first Causeway.

Reform mayor: Chep Morrison rode a wave of reform into City Hall but failed three times to ride into the State House as governor.

In 1956, Morrison collided with Earl Long in the governor's race. Earl shot him down in the country, calling him "Delesoops," referring to his television makeup and "toopee," and his fancy dress. "Them hunnerd dollar suits old Delesoops wears—they'd never fit ole Earl. Why, they'd look like socks on a rooster."

Rationality has never been a great asset in Louisiana politics. Earl Long's final tour as governor included side trips to western gambling casinos, New Orleans strip joints, and mental hospitals in Texas and southern Louisiana. His physical and mental health deteriorated almost daily before the eyes of television viewers; gradually, inexorably he came unhinged, haranguing the legislature with incoherent speeches, reviling legislators and swigging spirits freely from a soft drink bottle on the House floor.

Long's distraught family moved to get him treatment out of the spotlight. Earl wound up in Mandeville where he fired the head of the state mental hospital, then appointed someone who would discharge him. His wife Blanche, his political alter ego, eventually left him. In 1960, Earl, unable to succeed himself as governor, insisted on running one more campaign. He took on the incumbent congressman from his home District, Harold McSween, suffered a heart attack on election day, and still beat him. Two days later, Congressman-elect Earl Long died a winner.

Chep Morrison was Mayor of New Orleans for 16 years. Three times he ran unsuccessfully for governor, but was never able to overcome the Long mystique and the historic rejection by northern Louisiana of New Orleans Catholic candidates. President John Kennedy appointed him Ambassador to the Organization of American States. Morrison was beaten again in the 1964 gubernatorial primary, his final race. The winner, symbolically, was John McKeithen, whose racist campaign contrasted sharply with his moderation once in office. McKeithen, called "The New Type Long," was a protégé of Blanche Long, Uncle Earl's widow. Four months after his defeat, on May 22, 1964, Chep Morrison crashed enroute to Mexico in a light plane, and died with his son Randy.

Changing Order: For many years, gambling ran wide open in New Orleans. People played "the numbers" illegally for 40 years after the Louisiana Lottery was shut down by the federal government. The neighborhood bookie was as well known, and visible, as the cop on the beat.

When Chep Morrison rode a wave of reform into City Hall, after World War II, gambling pretty much skiddooed to Jefferson Parish. There were several swank clubs strung out along the old Jefferson Road—Club Forest,

Southport, the Beverly (now home of a dinner theater). Slot machines were said to outnumber citizens, five to one. You could crank them at leisure in almost any grocery or drug store. Sheriff Frank (King) Clancy presided over this "Free State of Jefferson." Clancy owned a good part of the largely undeveloped area. People hunted rabbits where the Veterans and Causeway Boulevards now intersect, the commercial hub of today's booming "bedroom" parish.

In 1951, Senator Estes Kefauver of Tennessee, modeling his coonskin cap for reporters, arrived in New Orleans, to investigate gambling. His hearings were the first telecasts of U. S. Senate proceedings in history. At the hearings, Kefauver paraded a number of underworld types before the camera. When the Senator, warming up to run for president, suggested in his firm, fatherly way that Frank Clancy, colorful old-time sheriff of Jefferson Parish, close down any gambling he found, Clancy said: "Yessir, if I find it, I'll close it down." Clancy was as good as his word. He found it. And he closed it down.

The Kefauver hearings of 1951 were America's first televised Senate proceedings. They were arranged for public viewing by the author, and inspired a series of congressional shows.

In 1952, Colonel Francis Grevemberg, state superintendent of police, waged total war on gambling of any kind, everything from backroom poker games to fund-raising bingo conducted in village churchyards. Grevemberg was unimpeachably honest. "There's something else wrong with him," said Earl Long, "but I can't remember exactly what it is." Bingo survived the assault. For more than a century, it had been the most popular method of fundraising for Catholic churches and schools in south Louisiana. Today, bingo is still thriving and it's doubtful that anything short of a papal encyclical will abolish this time-honored local pastime.

There was a feeling of *déjà vu* in New Orleans when the first civil rights sit-ins took place in 1958. Integration of the city's buses and streetcars evoked memories of the first battle to desegregate the mule-drawn "star" cars following the Reconstruction Act of 1867. Blacks had demanded entrance to taverns, restaurants, theaters. Whites responded by salting soft drinks and lacing food with cayenne pepper. The first integration attempts failed because whites dared to defy the law, and eventually blacks found that the law could not secure their rights. In 1874, for instance, the White League decided to "purify" the schools which had been integrated by court order in 1870. Vigilantes went from school to school purging any child with even a sunburn. Blacks continued to battle until April 1877, when Reconstruction ended and 80 years of unrelenting segregation began.

A much more cosmopolitan, racially mixed New Orleans reacted differently in 1960. But the 1960 and 1964 statewide elections were shadowed by old-line racist hate-mongering. In both elections Jimmy Davis and John McKeithen used familiar "seg" approaches to defeat racial moderate Chep

Governor Jimmy Davis made a fortune as a hillbilly singer and composer. His "You Are My Sunshine" has been translated into at least 20 different languages.

A. Pontchartrain Causeway
B. Bonnet Carré Spillway
C. Superdome
D. NASA
E. Metairie
F. Author's House

Morrison. Leander Perez, champion of racial purity and boss of Plaquemines Parish, prodded Davis into five special legislative sessions. The first session was a futile last-ditch effort to "interpose" state law over federal. The panicky legislators passed 29 separate acts. Federal Judge J. Skelly Wright kept his court open every night to throw them out, one by one.

The final desegregation of New Orleans' public schools in November 1960 was accomplished in an atmosphere of remarkable calm. Except during the first week, when a few overwrought mothers turned out to heckle, it happened gracefully. New Orleans, it was pointed out, was the most racially intermixed city in the nation. Its Mediterranean style of life and shared customs, its rich ethnic mix, made it unique in Dixie.

By 1965, for the first time in 90 years, two Republicans were on the floor of the Louisiana House of Representatives. Eisenhower in 1956 and Goldwater in 1964 had carried the state. A Republican candidate, Charlton Lyons, polled 40 percent of the statewide vote against McKeithen. Something "was blowin' in the wind," and John McKeithen seized upon the moment.

A staunch segregationist, he became a moderate at a tense time, subverting violence at Bogalusa in 1965. Instead of "hitting the big boys," he undertook an industrial crusade. He pushed for a code of ethics and other progressive measures. Where division and fragmentation had been the old Long technique, McKeithen counseled reconciliation and unity.

New Orleans benefited from this "new politics" in one extraordinary way. McKeithen gave his personal endorsement to the Superdome in New Orleans, gambling his political future. On November 4, 1967, voters approved both the stadium and a second term for McKeithen.

The Superdome has been called, among other things, "the world's largest room," and, by some wags, "the Mushroom that Ate New Orleans." It covers almost 10 acres, rises 27 stories high, and is about one-third of a mile wide. It can accommodate everything from tennis matches to rock concerts, motorcycle races to trade shows. The National Basketball Association attendance record was set there. The Rolling Stones shattered the indoor concert record in the Superdome. It is the home of three pigeons and the New Orleans Saints National Football League team. The engineers who conceived and built this 21st-century mega-structure succeeded in solving a myriad of problems, but no one knows how to get the pigeons out.

In 1967, the New Orleans Saints introduced the city to big-time professional football with a flourish: The home team ran the first kickoff back 93 yards for a touchdown. The franchise was the result of a ceaseless, six-year campaign by Dave Dixon, whose fertile mind also dreamed up the Superdome. Dixon's dream was almost deflated in 1965 when a group of black

The world's biggest room:
The Superdome hosted the
Super Bowl in 1978 (Dallas
over Denver) and 1981
(Oakland over Phila-
delphia). The hometown
Saints lose here regularly.

players walked out on an American Football League All-Star game, protesting "discrimination." A young attorney for the National Association for the Advancement of Colored People wound up representing the city. A black from the Treme area, his name was Ernest (Dutch) Morial. He was so light-skinned that when he first entered the players' suite, massive Cookie Gilchrist, leader of the rebellion, bawled out, "Man, you ain't no nigger." No one dreamed, at the time, that Morial would be elected Mayor in 1978, the first black to hold that office.

The Saints became a marvel of consistency—they never once enjoyed a winning season. However, a rotund placekicker with a withered arm and half a foot, Tom Dempsey, booted a 63-yard field goal against Detroit, the longest in NFL history. The fans brought a boisterous Mardi Gras spirit to every contest, regardless of the outcome. They concluded an abysmal 1–15 season in 1980 wearing bags over their heads, disguised as (S)Aints.

The Mardi Gras Syndrome: New Orleans mayors have been a varied lot. When Chep Morrison left office in July 1961, a chirpy little guy with a wispy moustache and a gift for the *non sequitur* named Victor Schiro treated the city to two terms of smiling *status quo*. Actually, a new industrial business boom had started, and Schiro, a graduate from the aldermanic ranks, did nothing to disturb it. Opponents snappishly said he did nothing. But most voters liked the cheerful little man. They said he had attended everything in New Orleans twice, including at least 800 Carnival balls (*de rigeur* for a mayor). Folks still remember such admonitions as: "Don't believe any false rumors, unless you hear them from me." Schiro's re-election slogan was pure balm of Gilead: "If it's good for New Orleans, I'm for it."

Schiro was succeeded in 1970 by the first of a new breed of politician, Maurice (Moon) Landrieu. Landrieu's stock in trade was a computerized mind that churned out facts and figures with such dazzling facility that his personality seemed lost somewhere in the output. He antagonized the media, not very difficult to do, and the media in turn antagonized Moon Landrieu. Landrieu's understanding of urban realities and the racial issue left him open to waspish criticism as the white flight to suburbia made New Orleans more than 50 percent black. For the first time, blacks were brought into the political mainstream, and the tireless Landrieu successfully dealt for a better-than-fair share of the federal dollar. Under the Carter administration, he became Secretary of Housing and Urban Development.

"The Mardi Gras syndrome" is a term coined by University of New Orleans professor James Bobo in the 1960s. It was applied to the drain on the city's economy and creative energies by an overgrown Carnival. Mardi Gras has expanded tremendously from a small folkfest, dominated by old-line social clubs, to a Brobdingnagian exercise in self-indulgence lasting more than two months and featuring upwards of 200 balls and 60 street parades. Bobo theorized it siphoned off too much money from investment in the real economy, leaving the city debilitated. Some natives suggested it might be better if Dr. Bobo simply left the city. Eventually he did, and became vice chancellor at Southern Alabama University.

The first two and a half weeks of May are now noisy with a jazz festival that is virtually an extension of Carnival. It started out as a small, somewhat classy, concert-style jazz event in 1970. By mid-decade it grew into a full-blown, tent-style festival at the Fair Grounds.

The jazz ranges widely, from gospel and Dixieland to Latin and progressive.

Somehow, the Mardi Gras spirit invades even the most serious endeavors. Few approaches to jurisprudence have been as cavalier as the three-ring circus initiated by the city's six-foot-six-inch district attorney, Jim Garrison, in 1967. He started with a flourish, calmly announcing that he had probably solved the assassination of John F. Kennedy. Then, assured of international attention, Garrison indicted one of the city's most prominent and successful businessmen, Clay Shaw, on charges of conspiracy.

Noted for his sardonic wit and flair for the classical allusion, Jim Garrison explained that it was all like Alice in Wonderland: "Black is white, and white is black." Of course, it also got "curiouser and curiouser." One witness, a junkie, told of seeing Shaw meet a contact on the lakefront while the junkie was shooting up on heroin. The key witness placed Shaw in a meeting which he "remembered" only after having been hypnotized, at Garrison's suggestion.

Clay Shaw, a strapping former World War II major, had served with distinction as executive director of International House. He was one of the prime movers in restoring the French Quarter, where he lived. But for two years Garrison kept the investigation going, patching together a mishmash of hearsay, rumor, and conjecture, while Clay Shaw dangled on his judicial string. On March 1, 1969, exactly two years to the day after his arrest, Clay Shaw was acquitted. The jury took less than 50 minutes to reach its decision.

In the face of crushing debts and disrepute, Shaw tried gamely to pick up the pieces, even after Garrison indicted him again, for perjury, to no purpose. On August 15, 1974, Clay Shaw died at the age of 61. In 1978 Jim Garrison was elected judge of the Louisiana Court of Appeals for the Fourth Circuit.

Who killed JFK? DA Jim Garrison said he knew, but three years of investigation and prosecution didn't prove a thing.

The Modern City: The French Quarter is a natural haven for artists and writers. A literary magazine, *The Double Dealer,* published the early work of William Faulkner, Ernest Hemingway, and Sherwood Anderson in the 1920s. Tennessee Williams lived in the Quarter, drawing inspiration for *A Streetcar Named Desire* and short stories like "Lord Byron's Love Letters." Truman Capote was another resident of the Vieux Carré.

In the thirties, Lyle Saxon headed a fertile WPA Writers Project which produced the excellent *New Orleans Guide* and its offshoot, *Gumbo Ya Ya,* rich in folklore. Saxon worked tirelessly to reawaken consciousness of the Vieux Carré as a living historical treasure. It needed doing. Chartres Street had become a jumble, Decatur a jungle, and Bourbon Street was in danger of becoming a slum. Royal Street maintained a kind of shoddy integrity.

The commercial awakening to the value of this unique city-within-a-city probably dates back to the survey made by the Real Estate Research Bureau of Chicago in the mid-1950s. This landmark report states: "The French Quarter represents the largest day-in, day-out concentration of out-of-town visitors that exists anywhere in the United States."

The man who first utilized the potential of the old town was Edgar Stern, Jr. In December 1948 he built the city's first television studio, WDSU-TV, smack in the middle of the French Quarter, carefully adhering to the Vieux Carré Commission's codes. It was practically invisible to pedestrians, screened by the 1819 elegance of the old Seignoret mansion and courtyard at 520 Royal Street. Later, he constructed the elegant Royal Orleans Hotel, on the same spot where the St. Louis once catered to the *crème de la crème.*

Suddenly, the historical Vieux Carré was rediscovered. The Vieux Carré Commission, bolstered legally by each test of its sovereignty, protects the integrity of the old city, approves repairs and remodeling of its buildings, and

Canal Street, 1981: One of the widest streets in the world is now overshadowed by tall buildings.

New Orleans' future as an ocean-going port was assured in 1880 by Captain James B. Eads. Historically, ships had waited weeks, sometimes months, to pass the shallow river's mouth. Eads designed a series of jetties that deepened the channel and opened a permanent passage to the world. On undertaking the job, Eads promised "No cure, No pay", and more than earned his $10 million.

ensures the preservation of the whole. Unlike Williamsburg and other planned restorations, the Vieux Carré is a "living city" 24 hours a day, not just a museum piece or carefully crafted tourist attraction. Year-round residents still make their homes where Bienville and Claiborne, opera diva Adelina Patti, chess genius Paul Morphy, and Tennessee Williams lived.

One of the most dramatic preservationist battles ever fought, sometimes called the Second Battle of New Orleans, was contested here in the 1960s. In 1956, the federal government embarked on the $100-billion, 42,500-mile interstate highway system. A mammoth six-lane, 108-foot-wide, 40-foot-high elevated expressway was proposed for New Orleans. It would sweep down over part of the Quarter and pass directly in front of Jackson Square, obliterating the classic riverfront view of Bienville's "beautiful crescent."

Led by William Long, owner of the *Vieux Carré Courier,* architect Mark Lowrey, and preservationist Martha Robinson, local citizens mounted an intensive campaign to "stop the Highwaymen." Finally, in June 1969, Transportation Secretary John Volpe canceled the Vieux Carré expressway.

New Orleans has managed to conquer the swamp, control and direct the river, and build a towering metropolis on one side of Canal Street while preserving the historic ambiance of its venerable Vieux Carré. This municipal balancing act continues into the 1980s, with some futurists predicting that New Orleans' greatest era of growth will come during the next two decades.

Tourism and the port are its two great industries. For two centuries, New Orleans has been one of the world's great ports. It currently ranks second to New York in most categories, but its future is almost limitless. It is becoming, in a sense, one huge extended port, reaching well into the Gulf of Mexico.

A giant, ultramodern complex called Centroport is being constructed along the Gulf outlet below the city. It will take 30 years to complete. When it is finished in the year 2000, much of the city's current wharfage will have been antiquated and replaced by a combination of residential and recreational facilities.

Since the Superdome was completed, unprecedented downtown construction has caused the skyline to change radically, especially along the Poydras corridor. The year 1980 saw eight new office buildings either completed or under construction, averaging 27 stories in height, a total investment of $193 million.

More and more, the energy business is becoming the third major factor in New Orleans' economy. The Louisiana Offshore Port (LOOP), the nation's first "superport," eventually will supply one million barrels of oil a day to refineries as far away as Chicago and Buffalo. New Orleans is headquarters for the world's largest supplier of marine services for offshore oil. It is the largest builder of supply vessels and deck barges in the world. The great delta swamp, once its enemy, has become the city's provider.

Tourism's growth is astounding. The city played host to over six million visitors in 1980. More than 800 conventions were held in New Orleans. Ten years ago, there were fewer than 4,000 first-class hotel rooms downtown. Now there are more than 20,000; many more are planned.

It is as if Louisiana and, to some extent, New Orleans had awakened from a lengthy industrial slumber. The state led the nation in industrial expansion and new industry in 1977–1981. In a flight over the river corridor between New Orleans and Baton Rouge today, a striking pattern can be seen. Strung out in an almost unbroken line is a giant industrial complex — oil refineries, grain elevators, petrochemical plants — graphic evidence of how the Isle of Orleans has broken free of its historic swampland isolation.

Traditionally the river has been the great provider and the great destroyer. As long as Ole Man River remained untamed, New Orleans was fated to be vulnerable. The city's final triumph is a tribute to the consistently heroic efforts of the United States Army Corps of Engineers, which since 1803 has played an ever-increasing role in adapting the delta to man's needs and demands. The Corps opened the streams to commerce, protected farmlands and cities from flooding, shored up, contained, and diverted the river. The Bonnet Carré Spillway, completed in 1937, has twice been opened above New Orleans to siphon off potential floods.

Until recently, almost one-third of the area within the city limits was virtually uninhabitable, populated mostly by fish, turtles, alligators, and *poules d'eau*. Now the 12,000-acre Almonester Corridor, the city's first industrial park, is projected for the turn of the century, bringing with it 50,000 new jobs. Not far away the National Aeronautics and Space Administration established the Michoud Assembly Facility in 1961. The giant Saturn booster rockets that powered the spacecraft which reached the moon were produced there. More recently, the huge fuel tanks that feed the space shuttle were built at Michoud.

As this book was going to press New Orleans was gearing up for an AA-size (bigger than Knoxville, smaller than Montreal) world's fair in 1984. The site is the old warehouse district between the Mississippi River Bridge and Canal Street. Appropriately, the fair's theme is the River and how it has affected New Orleans. Eleven million visitors are expected.

Mistress and Wife: New Orleans has weathered the transitions and sometimes the transgressions of six different governments. It subdivided itself into three different cities between 1836 and 1851. And it was occupied, a prisoner of the United States of America, for 15 more years during and after the Civil War.

For almost a century, this "most European of all American cities" flew a foreign flag and spoke a foreign language. Figuratively the Isle of Orleans, it was the nearest thing to a culturally independent island state that this nation had ever seen. In fact, when the Americans first arrived, the Creoles considered them interlopers rather than liberators, occupiers instead of partners.

Mediterranean by heritage, climate, and attitude, island Orleans is a cultural enclave. It developed its own cuisine, its own architecture, its own patois, and its own special festival, Mardi Gras. Its laws were, in some cases, unique in the United States: the Code Noir, the Code Duello, the Napoleonic Code (still the basis of most Louisiana civil law). In contending with recurrent disaster, its people developed a special genius for celebration. "We are so fond of life," the Creoles explained, "we have no leisure to entertain the terror of dying." It was no accident that jazz and the jazz funeral evolved in New Orleans; death only served to enhance life's raptures.

Most Orleanians view their city in a familial, quite personal way. The city has a beguiling personality, a contagious warmth, an unaffected character reflected in its many nicknames—Big Easy, the City That Care Forgot, the Queen City of the South, the Paris of the Americas—that affection invariably involves analogies to food or love. The late jazzman Oscar (Papa) Celestin once told me: "Man, if I likes Noo Awlins anymo', I eats Noo Awlins up." The Creoles summed up their romance with the city, saying: "She'd have been my choice as mistress if I hadn't married her."

Today there are still two cities—one two centuries old, a French city built almost entirely by the Spanish, then rebuilt by the Americans in a style distinctly their own. The other is skyscraper modern, some of it only a few weeks old, rushing headlong into the future. The scene has changed dramatically in the last decade. The Vieux Carré, the Garden District, Coliseum Square, and other historic areas have become tangible assets, cash-convertible in terms of the gigantic tourist business. Those six million visitors are generally not interested in touring skyscrapers. On the whole, tourism is the business that has finally fused the efforts of both the progressive and the preservationist. Mardi Gras, for all its raucous self-indulgence, has become a billion-dollar business. The city still has a relatively small middle class and remains socially stratified as few other cities are, although it is probably more truly integrated than any city in the nation.

Modern Mardi Gras, meanwhile, is becoming less a tradition than a party. It's a kind of mass therapy that eases community tensions; in fact, it may be the one annealing force that regularly brings the entire city together. Even the uptown social set, which once dominated Carnival in a spirit of haughty *noblesse oblige,* has kept an identity, a neighborhood, that works against the suburban exodus. For the first time in two decades, people who fled integration and urban blight are coming back to the city.

William Makepeace Thackeray, the great English writer, visited New Orleans in the mid-19th century, and wrote an encomium on Creole cuisine that is cherished to this day by local restaurateurs. "This old Franco Spanish city on the banks of the Mississippi . . . where, of all the cities in the world, you can eat the most and suffer the least, where the claret is as good as in Bordeaux, and where a ragout and a bouillabaise can be the like of which was never even in Marseilles or Paris."

A Short History of New Orleans

"The more things change, the more they stay the same." This most enduring of all Creole French sayings reflects a society, a race, and a city wedded to custom and too often captive to tradition. But in many ways, this is no longer true. The city and the state, virtual strangers to democratic government until 1920, have recently leaped into genuine two-party politics, though some of the old *sauce piquante* quality of the Longs and Perezes still remains. New Orleans' traditional suspicion of outsiders is fading, although some natives still insist that one can't really be considered a "native" until he's resided in the city a quarter of a century. There may always be a built-in resistance to change, a conservative inertia, a tendency toward a *mañana* philosophy. But that is precisely the languid charm of this subtropical city whose value system is not yet oriented exclusively to efficiency or speed.

New Orleans faces most of the serious problems that burden modern American municipalities: housing blight and urban decay, rising crime rates, lack of a vital tax base. Because of its delayed start on a public school system, the inadequacy of education remains a serious drawback to the full realization of its human potential. In this respect, traditional French *laissez faire* makes collective solutions harder. But as someone said: "It is easier to live in New Orleans on a little than anywhere else in the country on a lot." Any city that makes a banquet out of red beans and rice knows how to make the most of things.

Ironically, New Orleans is referred to as a Creole city even though the Creoles don't run it, haven't been really influential for over 100 years, and have no great wealth, power, or identity left. It is even difficult to find two Creoles who agree on exactly what a Creole is. They constantly write argumentative letters to the newspapers, haggling over definitions. It is a kind of futile shadow-boxing with the past.

Creole, as a meaningful term, no longer defines a nationality or breed. Creole has become a special attitude toward life. Auntie Mame was a Creole, I suspect. Her famous proclamation, "Life is a banquet, and some damn fools are starving to death," is quintessential Creole New Orleans. So in New Orleans you find Creole Irish, Creole German, even Creole Chinese. Forget the Creole definitions, *mes amis*—in New Orleans, almost everyone has been happily Creolized for some time. *Bon appetit!*

Selected Bibliography

This is a partial list of books the author found helpful in developing this history of New Orleans. They might also serve the discriminating reader eager to learn more about certain aspects of the city's growth and culture. New Orleans is truly a "storybook town," and it thrives on mystery, legend, and intrigue. Generally the facts are more fun than the fiction. Admitting my infatuation with the place and its people, I tried to follow Mark Twain's dictum: "First get the facts; then you can distort them."

Cable, Mary. *Lost New Orleans*. Boston: Houghton Mifflin, 1980. A handsomely illustrated study of the city's social and cultural growth, its threatened and disappearing architecture.

Capers, Gerald. *Occupied City: New Orleans Under Federal Rule, 1862–1865*. Lexington: University of Kentucky Press, 1965. "Beast Butler" versus the "She-Adders," one of the lesser-known battles of the Civil War.

Carter, Hodding, ed. *The Past as Prelude—New Orleans, 1718–1968*. New Orleans: Tulane University Press, 1968. A 250th anniversary compendium of discerning essays on law, architecture, education, music, the arts, politics, Mardi Gras.

Chase, John. *Frenchmen, Desire, Good Children*. New York: Collier Books, 1979. A droll guide to the city, discussing its unusual street names and characters.

Christovich, M. L., and others. *New Orleans Architecture*. New Orleans: Friends of the Cabildo/Pelican Publishing, 1974–79. Six stunningly illustrated volumes expertly assembled; cemeteries are included.

Dufour, Charles L. *The Night the War Was Lost*. Garden City: Doubleday, 1960. The engrossing story of Farragut's capture of New Orleans in 1862.

Fortier, Alcee. *The History of Louisiana*, Vols. I and II. New York, 1904. Despite heavy bias, excellent insight into Spanish Era, annotated incisively by Mary Jo Corrigan.

Freiberg, Edna. *Bayou St. John in Colonial Louisiana, 1699–1803*. New Orleans: Harvey Press, 1980. The first full study of the initial settlement (1708) above Bienville's site, exhaustively researched.

Huber, Leonard. *Tales of the Mississippi*. New York: Hastings House, 1955. An illustrated, anecdotal history of the steamboat era.

Kane, Harnett. *Louisiana Hayride: The American Rehearsal for Dictatorship*. New Orleans: Pelican Publishing, 1970. This journalistic piledriver documents the systematic plundering of a 20th-century American state.

A Short History of New Orleans

Kirkwood, James. *American Grotesque*. New York: Simon and Schuster, 1968. An agonizingly factual account of Jim Garrison's bizarre witch-hunt and how it destroyed an innocent man.

Saxon, Lyle. *Fabulous New Orleans*. New York, 1928. Unabashedly romantic, admittedly subjective, this enchanting portrait of New Orleans is still delightful reading.

Soniat, Leon. *La Bouche Creole*. Gretna: Pelican Publishing, 1980. This unique cookbook is authentic Creole, filled with excursions into Creole folklore, customs, sayings, and personal reminiscences.

Tallant, Robert. *Voodoo in New Orleans*. New York: Collier Books, 1962. The foremost authority on the history and growth of "that awful religion" in New Orleans.

Taylor, Joe G. *Louisiana: A Bicentennial History*. New York: W. W. Norton, 1976. The ideal introduction to state and local history by a recognized authority. One hundred eighty-six concise, sharply written pages, from La Salle to Edwin Edwards.

—————. *Louisiana Reconstructed: 1863–1877*. Baton Rouge: Louisiana State University Press, 1974. The definitive work on the Reconstruction in Louisiana; a reasoned, lucid account of one of America's most perplexing periods.

Williams, T. Harry. *Huey Long*. New York: Alfred A. Knopf, 1971. A historian presents the life of Huey Long in a volume using oral history as its principal source material which won a well-deserved Pulitzer prize.

PICTURE CREDITS

City Art Museum of St. Louis, Mo.: 54

Rick Day: 140, 149, 152

Historic New Orleans Collection: Cover, 6, 11, 13, 15, 20, 28, 33 (right), 40, 45, 46, 59, 63, 66, 68–69, 73, 78, 82, 86, 91, 96, 101, 102, 104, 107, 109, 114, 118, 120, 121, 125, 130, 133, 135, 138

Mel Leavitt: 143, 146, 151

Louisiana State Museum: 60

New Orleans Public Library: 116

Office of the Mayor of New Orleans, Public Information Office: 22, 75

Ursuline Convent, New Orleans: 33 (left)

Index

Note: Page numbers in italics refer to illustrations.

A Short History of New Orleans